Kathleen M. Goad BA

Brodie's N

Persuasion

Pan Educational London and Sydney

Contents

The author iii

The book
As a novel 1
Plot 2
Theme 4
Setting 5
Characters 7
Style 27
Humour 33
Suitability for radio, stage and cinema 35

The novel before Jane Austen 37

Summaries of chapters, textual notes and revision questions 39

General questions 53

Context questions 55

Key to context questions 58

First published by James Brodie Ltd
This edition published 1976 by Pan Books Ltd,
Cavaye Place, London SW10 9PG
5 6 7 8 9

ISBN 0 330 50025 2
Printed and bound in Great Britain by
Richard Clay (The Chaucer Press) Ltd, Bungay, Suffolk

The author

Jane Austen was born on 16 December 1775 at Steventon, in Hampshire, where her father, George Austen, was rector. He also ran a farm and coached a few pupils in order to get money to provide for his large family of six boys and two girls. Her mother, in spite of persistent illness, had a keen and lively mind and greatly appreciated a joke. The eldest of the family was James, who later became rector of Steventon in his father's place; next came Edward, who was adopted while young by Mr and Mrs Knight of Godmersham in Kent, who were distant cousins. Then there was Henry, with whom Jane seems to have been most in sympathy and who went into business later on, but became bankrupt. Francis, another brother, and Charles, the youngest, served in the Navy and rose to be admirals. Cassandra, Jane's only sister, was two years her senior, and as the girls grew up they became inseparable. It was a very happy family, and one feels that the Christmas scene at Uppercross when the Musgrove children were home for the holidays is probably described from actual memory. Little is recorded of Jane's babyhood except that she lived with a nurse in Steventon and played with the children of the villagers, which was the custom of the time. In 1782 the two sisters paid a visit to some relatives of their mother and soon afterwards Cassandra was sent to the Abbey School in Reading, where Jane soon followed her since, as her mother said, 'If Cassandra were going to have her head cut off, Jane would insist on sharing her fate.' Perhaps this school was like the one at Exeter where the Musgrove girls had acquired their accomplishments, or that described by Emma, 'a real honest old-fashioned boarding-school, where a reasonable quantity of accomplishments were sold at a reasonable price and where girls might be sent to be out of the way and scramble themselves into a little education without any danger of coming back prodigies'. Two years later they were home again, continuing their education by listening to their father as he read his favourite poems to his pupils, drawing up reading lists, and reading French and perhaps Italian with their cousin, Eliza Hancock, who married first a Frenchman, the Comte de Feuillide, and later, when he had been guillotined by the French Republican government during the Reign of Terror, became the wife of Jane's brother, Henry. They also enjoyed the private theatricals which Eliza sometimes planned. The girls acquired a liking for the works of Shakespeare, Dr Johnson, Cowper and Goldsmith during these years, and later on Jane read many novels, including those of Fanny Burney, Fielding, Richardson, and later still the novels of mystery of Horace Walpole and Mrs Radcliffe and the fine historical novels of Sir Walter Scott. She was a lively girl at this time who loved dancing and music and pleasure of all kinds. In appearance she is said to have been attractive, tall and slender with a good complexion, hazel eyes and curly brown hair. Her manner was quiet and she preferred to listen to the conversation of others rather than talk much herself. Troubles soon came to the family; her brother James's wife died, and his little daughter came to Steventon to be looked after; Cassandra suffered a great grief when the man she was to marry died suddenly. All these things strengthened Jane's character and made her more sympathetic. Long before Rev. and Mrs Austen decided to move from Steventon to Bath in 1801, Jane had begun to scribble, as she called it, and in 1796 she had begun her first book which she called *First Impressions*. This she sent to a publisher who thought so little of it that he sent it back by return of post. When she revised it and sent if off again sixteen years later, it was an immediate success as *Pride and Prejudice*. She used to write in the sitting-room she shared with Cassandra and the others, and read her work aloud to amuse the family. This may account for much of the fluency of her style, for there is nothing like reading aloud for perfecting a piece of writing. It is said that she would slip the pieces of paper on which she was writing under a book if she was disturbed, and that at one time she refused to have a creaking door attended to since it warned her of the approach of visitors. One of her nieces tells us that she continued to write even when she was on a visit to her brother's house. She would sit quietly by the fire sewing for a while then, suddenly, she would burst out laughing, run to the table where the pens and paper were kept, write something down and afterwards go back to her work. At first, like Anne Elliot, Jane hated the idea of leaving the country for Bath, but she consoled herself with the prospect of travelling, which materialized when the family visited Sidmouth, Dawlish, Ramsgate and Lyme Regis in successive years. It was during one of these visits, it seems, that Jane probably met someone with whom she fell in love but who died soon after the meeting. It was possibly partly because of this sorrow and partly because of the sorrow at her father's death in 1805 that she wrote nothing, so far as we know, from 1804 to 1811. In 1807 Mrs Austen and her daughters settled at Southampton with Francis Austen, and from there the younger women paid frequent visits to their various brothers. In 1808 Edward Austen, who had changed his name to Knight when he was adopted, and who now inherited his cousins' large estates, found himself a widower with a large family. He was glad of the help of his sisters and soon offered his mother a house at Chawton on his Hampshire estate. This was an ideal place for the three women since it was convenient for all the young nephews and nieces to visit when they came to stay at the Great House. Here Jane took up her writing again, revising the old manuscripts which had been put away so many years before, and began new ones. The first book to be published, in 1811, was *Sense and Sensibility*, then came *Pride and Prejudice* in 1813 and *Mansfield Park* in 1814. Jane was now becoming famous, and while *Emma*, published in 1815, was still in the press, she received a letter from the Prince Regent's librarian giving her permission to dedicate 'any future work' to the Prince. In 1817 came *Persuasion*, and in 1818 *Susan*, which she had finished as long before as 1799 and sold to a publisher in 1803, at last appeared as *Northanger Abbey*; both these books were published after her death. Jane's last complete novel, *Persuasion*, was written under great difficulties, for she had to nurse first her mother, and then Henry; soon after she was still more depressed when Henry became bankrupt. These troubles affected her own health, but she went on working at another novel which her family called

Sanditon and which, like an earlier work, *The Watsons*, she left unfinished. At last she became so much worse that Cassandra took her to Winchester to consult a doctor. Unfortunately he could do little for her, and it was there, in lodgings on 18 July 1817, that she died. She was buried in Winchester Cathedral.

The book

As a novel

Before attempting to assess the value of a novel it is first necessary to decide to which class it belongs, for novels may be divided into four classes. The first kind is the novel of action or adventure, in which exciting events follow each other in quick succession. Scott's novels are of this kind, and so are those of Henry Fielding, Robert Louis Stevenson and John Buchan. The second kind is the novel of character in which the people are more important than the plot, and the adventures which befall them are designed to show them to the best advantage. *Pickwick Papers* is one of the best examples of this type. The name *picaresque* is sometimes applied to this kind of novel when the hero moves from one adventure to another with not much connection between them. Next comes the modern and very difficult type of novel of which, perhaps, Virginia Woolf's work gives the best examples. Her book *Mrs. Dalloway* tries to give the reader the thoughts and ideas – 'the stream of consciousness' – in a woman's mind as she goes shopping for her birthday party, and in so doing to suggest her past experiences as well as her hopes and fears for the future. Finally comes the dramatic novel in which character and action are almost equally important and so blended that it is impossible to think of one without the other. All Jane Austen's books belong to this last group.

Having decided to which class a novel belongs, it is then necessary to consider it with regard to certain qualities by which its merits may be judged. First and most important comes movement or pace; the story must pass from one happening to the next and the reader should be made to feel that the rate at which it moves is fitting to the subject. In *Persuasion*, as in all Jane Austen's books, the movement is slow, for she is depicting a leisurely kind of life in which people are seldom in a hurry. Since she is a great artist, however, she varies the pace very skilfully in order to increase the tension at moments of stress as when Anne discovers Mr Elliot's true character. Secondly, the development of character must be studied.

People grow wiser and saner, or they become bitter and disgruntled as they suffer the trials of life, and the good novelist shows the effect of experience on the people introduced. Anne Elliot has become more sympathetic and tolerant because of her early disappointment in love, while Elizabeth's selfishness has increased with her stay at Bath. Very important, too, is the author's attitude to life. All great works of art help the reader to understand life a little better, and although Jane Austen makes us laugh, there is a deep seriousness behind the laughter. She makes us realize how foolish it was that a woman with Anne Elliot's gifts should be condemned to a futile existence with her selfish father and sister. The setting of the story and the style of the writing also demand careful attention.

Plot

Persuasion is the story of Anne Elliot, the second daughter of Sir Walter Elliot of Kellynch Hall in Somerset. Seven years before the story opens, Anne had fallen in love with Captain Frederick Wentworth, an intelligent but poor naval officer, and had become engaged to him. Her father had disapproved of the match but this would not necessarily have prevented it; when, however, her great friend and adviser, Lady Russell, who had been her dead mother's friend, also spoke strongly against it, urging that it would be imprudent and might be unfortunate for Captain Wentworth as well as for herself, Anne broke the engagement, whereupon her lover left the country feeling resentful at the way in which he had been treated.

When the story begins, Sir Walter, who is a vain and stupid man, finds himself so heavily in debt that he must learn to live on a less lavish scale. He is very unwilling to let Kellynch Hall, but is eventually persuaded by his agent, Mr Shepherd, and Lady Russell, that Admiral and Mrs Croft would be desirable tenants. At length the business is arranged, and just before the removal takes place, Anne discovers, to her embarrassment that Mrs Croft is the sister of Captain Wentworth.

Sir Walter and his eldest daughter, Elizabeth, who is as proud and as vain as her father, now set out for Bath, accompanied by Mrs Clay, the widowed daughter of Mr Shepherd, while Anne goes to visit her other sister, Mary. Mary is married to Charles Musgrove, who had first proposed to Anne and had been refused by her, and has two little boys. She lives at Uppercross Cottage in the grounds of the Great House where her husband's family dwell. Anne likes homely Mrs Musgrove, senior, and her husband, and finds life at Uppercross preferable to that at Bath. It is not long before Admiral and Mrs Croft begin to pay calls in the neighbourhood and, naturally they come to the Great House. Mrs Croft talks of her brother who, Mrs Musgrove discovers, was once in command of a ship on which her scapegrace son, Dick Musgrove, now dead, had served. Anne dreads meeting Captain Wentworth, and for a while succeeds in avoiding him. Mary's little boy has an accident and this enables Anne to stay away from the Great House for a while. At last, however, he comes to the Cottage and she sees him again. The situation is not as awkward as she had imagined it would be, and she accepts it calmly. Mary's two sisters-in-law, Henrietta and Louisa Musgrove, are very delighted with Captain Wentworth, and he is so constantly in their company that Anne imagines he is in love with one of them. During a morning walk in the autumn, however, she realizes that Henrietta is in love with her cousin, Charles Hayter, a young curate, of whom the snobbish Mary disapproves.

Captain Wentworth now pays a visit to his friend, Captain Harville, at Lyme Regis, and when the Musgrove girls hear of this, they, too, want to visit this town. An excursion is arranged, during which several important events occur. First they meet a Captain Benwick, who was engaged to Captain Harville's sister who has recently died. Next they see Mr Elliot, a distant cousin, who is Sir Walter's heir, and thirdly Louisa falls on the Cobb and is seriously hurt. For a while Anne is involved in the misfortunes of the family at Uppercross, but soon she has to pay her promised visit to Lady Russell and then go to Bath to live with her father and sister. Here she finds herself in a completely different and less congenial world. Sir Walter has taken a house in Camden Street where he and Elizabeth entertain the society of the city. Mrs Clay is still with them, acting as companion to Elizabeth, but Anne fears that she may be hoping to persuade Sir Walter to marry her. Mr Elliot, Sir Walter's heir, whom Anne had seen at Lyme, is a frequent visitor to the house. He has had no connections with Sir Walter and his family for many years previously because of his marriage to a wealthy but low-born woman. Now, however, his wife has recently died and he is anxious to renew his acquaintance with his cousins, and, if possible, to prevent Sir Walter from getting married again. Anne is at first pleased to see him because she thinks he will marry Elizabeth, but it is soon obvious that it is Anne herself whom he admires. Meanwhile she learns, to her surprise, that Captain Benwick and Louisa Musgrove, who have been thrown into each other's company a great deal during Louisa's convalescence, have fallen in love and become engaged. This means, of course, that Captain Wentworth can no longer hope to marry Louisa, but Anne is assured by Admiral Croft, who has now arrived in Bath with his wife, that the captain seems in no way disturbed. Not long after this Anne meets Captain Wentworth on several occasions and begins to hope that he may still be in love with her. She also realizes Mr Elliot's intentions towards herself, partly through an old schoolfellow with whom she has resumed friendship. This lady, Mrs Smith, who is now a widow with little money and in poor health, has known Mr Elliot in his younger days, and she tells Anne of his callousness and lack of generosity. Anne is troubled about these matters, but presently her attention is distracted from them by the arrival in Bath of her sister, Mary, and most of the Musgrove family. Henrietta Musgove is to marry her cousin, Charles Hayter, and has come to Bath to buy her trousseau. Anne now knows that she has nothing to fear from either of the Musgrove girls, and soon after, when she is visiting Mrs Musgrove at her hotel, Captain Wentworth gives her a letter in which he declares that he has always loved her. And so the story ends with the marriage of Anne and her lover, the altered circumstances of the captain having persuaded Sir Walter and Lady Russell, who had originally objected to the match, to change their minds.

Theme

Persuasion is a presentation of the life of those people among whom Jane Austen herself lived. Most of them belonged to the lesser aristocracy or the upper middle class, had comfortable incomes and spent the greater part of their time in visiting or entertaining. Many of them were snobs with an exaggerated respect for rank and position. The novel is more than this, however, for it tells how the daughter of a proud family was persuaded by her father's attitude and by the efforts of a well-meaning friend to refuse to marry an impecunious naval officer with whom she was in love; how bitterly she regretted this action and what her life became as the unmarried daughter of the family; and how, finally, when the officer had become wealthy and distinguished, her relatives and friends were persuaded to approve of him at last.

Setting

This novel is set in the south of England in 1814 and gives a vivid picture of the life of the upper middle class at that time. As in *Pride and Prejudice* the vulgar Mrs Bennet, who was of lower rank than her husband, valued money above all things, so in this book Sir Walter Elliot and two of his daughters value rank as the most important thing in the world, and even sensible Lady Russell has 'a value for rank and consequence which blinded her a little to the faults of those who possessed them'.

When the story opens, we are shown what life was like in the country, at Kellynch Hall and at Uppercross. None of the men seems to have much to do; Sir Walter spends most of his time amusing himself, and his only reading is *The Baronetage*, which soothes his vanity. At Uppercross Mr Musgrove and his son 'had their own game to guard and to destroy, their own horses, dogs and newspapers to engage them'; in other words hunting, riding and shooting kept them tolerably busy at times. When Charles married, he did not leave his father's estate, but only moved to one of the farmhouses which had been converted into a cottage for him and his wife. Women were even more restricted in their activities, and had more time to spare, than the men. They were always interested in 'housekeeping, neighbours, dress, dancing and music', Jane Austen tells us. Both men and women formed walking parties and spent autumn days strolling through the country lanes in groups. At night the families in the neighbourhood entertained each other to dinner and to impromptu parties, at which the daughters sang or played the piano or harp, and there was country dancing. When this was at the

Musgrove's house, Anne played for the dancing all the time because she preferred to do this rather than dance. Above all they talked, and many of their long, leisurely and sometimes tedious conversations are recorded for us. At Christmas time there were many happy family parties like that at Uppercross where, when Anne and Lady Russell called before setting out for Bath, we are told: 'On one side was a table occupied by some chattering girls, cutting up silk and gold paper; and on the other were tressels and trays, bending under the weight of brawn and cold pies, where riotous boys were holding high revel; the whole completed by a roaring Christmas fire, which seemed determined to be heard in spite of all the noise of the others.' In days of few schools and slow transport the children were sent away to be educated at boarding-schools; Louisa and Henrietta Musgrove had just returned from such a school at Exeter where they had acquired the 'stock accomplishments'; the younger Musgrove children were still away. Anne was educated at a similar school for it was there that she knew Mrs Smith, then Miss Hamilton, who was very kind to her. Evidently Anne had happy memories of her schooldays, for she had taken the trouble to keep in touch with one of the teachers, whom she visited at Bath. When they left school, the girls did not train for careers, of course, but returned home to wait until they found husbands, and the position of the girl who did not marry was far from enviable. Women were always under the authority of some male relative, usually husband or father, unless they became widows, when they were allowed to have some control of their own affairs. Most families of consequence gave their daughters the benefit of a few weeks in London each spring to enjoy the pleasures of the world of fashion, but with the Elliot family it seems to have been only Elizabeth, the eldest daughter, who received this advantage.

Next to London in importance with the ladies and gentlemen of quality came Bath, where those who were really ill and those who only thought themselves ill, came to take the waters and to meet their friends. They travelled by carriage or curricle, and as it was usually in the winter that they made these migrations, the journeys must have been extremely tedious. Travelling on Sunday was considered to be very wrong. Occasionally, of course, expeditions, like the ill-fated one to Lyme, were made, and ladies bathed at the seaside. During these visits they stayed at inns like the White Hart at Bath.

Life in Bath was much more varied than life in the country for both men and women. By day the men drank the waters and had their guns and other sporting equipment repaired, while the ladies went shopping to match ribbons or change their library books. At night, there were many amusements – the theatre, concerts, dances, and gaiety for everyone. The conventions were strictly observed, with much homage paid to rank and wealth, order of precedence, formal calls and the leaving of cards. Ladies curtsied when they met friends. Dress was most important, but the book gives us few details, except for frequent mention of pelisses. Ladies wore hats out of doors and caps indoors (XV).

The reader is also given glimpses of yet a third kind of life, the life of naval officers and their wives who have left the sea either temporarily, like Captain Wentworth, or permanently, like Admiral Croft, and come to live amongst those who have travelled little. These are a race apart, intelligent, keen and very tender-hearted, in spite of occasional eccentricities. Their hard life at sea aged them prematurely, and made them more simple and direct than the landsmen. They had more subjects of conversation, too, and did not fit in with the world of fashion. The sailors' wives were accustomed to voyaging with their husbands and sharing the dangers of encounters with Napoleon's navy. Mrs Croft declares that the ships were very comfortable, especially the larger ones, and even in a frigate, although the travellers must of necessity be more confined, the accommodation was good. 'Any reasonable woman may be perfectly happy in one of them,' she says. Captain Wentworth, on the other hand, hated to see women on board, and reminded his sister that she was travelling with her husband as captain (VIII).

Characters *Anne Elliot*

A strong mind with sweetness of manner.

Anne Elliot is the kindest and most gentle of all Jane Austen's heroines. When the story begins she is already twenty-seven, an age which in the early nineteenth century meant that she was well past her youth and rapidly becoming one of those unattached women who look after their sisters' children, nurse the sick, and act as companions to elderly relatives. Jane Austen herself played this role in her own family, and so she portrays Anne's lot with sympathy and understanding. Anne is more unfortunate in her relatives than Jane was, however, since neither her father nor her sister, Elizabeth, has any thought or consideration for her. To them she is 'only Anne', and is expected always to do what they demand and to have no wishes of her own. Her father has never had any appreciation of her delicate beauty, and now that her early prettiness has somewhat faded, he considers her to be haggard. Her other sister, Mary, is almost as bad in her attitude, the only difference being that Anne is more useful to her. Lady Russell alone gives her the love she deserves. In spite of her family's lack of affection for her, however, and the loss of her lover, she is not embittered, and her sweetness of temper is shown at all times, notably when Mary Musgrove, returning from the Great House where she has met Captain Wentworth, repeats his remark to Henrietta that Anne had 'altered beyond recognition'. Although deeply mortified by what she imagines to be the meaning of this statement, Anne admits its justice and uses it to make herself forgo any romantic notions about her former lover. In this incident she also shows great strength of character.

Everyone in trouble turns naturally to Anne for help and sympathy, and in an emergency it is she who takes command of the situation. When the young Charles Musgrove falls and dislocates his collar-bone, it is Anne who sends for the apothecary and for her brother-in-law; she it is who looks after Mary, who is having hysterics, and directs the servants and the other child, as well as caring for the injured boy. It is Anne again who decides in every particular what is best to be done when Louisa is injured at Lyme, while Henrietta and Mary are so overcome that they faint. No one appeals to her for sympathy in vain; she is willing to listen to Mrs Musgrove's talk about her dead son, to look after little Charles while his mother and father dine at the Great House, to play the piano that the others may dance, and to visit poor, sick Mrs Smith, even when it means giving up an invitation from her family's rich relations.

She is no snob like her sisters, and dislikes both her father's fawning attentions to Lady Dalrymple and Mary's desire that everyone should acknowledge her rank. She is too intelligent for snobbery or stupid pride, and Captain Wentworth obviously has her in mind when he describes what he wants in a wife as 'a strong mind with sweetness of manner'. Her intelligence and her sweetness are both revealed also in her conversations with Captain Benwick.

Yet, in spite of her many virtues, there is nothing priggish or abnormal about her, and it is her naturalness which attracts on every occasion. She feels the secret pleasure that any woman would understand when Mr Elliot so clearly admires her at Lyme, although she does not know who he is. She has a keen sense of humour, too, although she is much too kind to take a malicious pleasure in other people's difficulties.

Above all else she is faithful and steadfast, particularly in her love for Captain Wentworth. She gave him up in her youth because she was persuaded that a marriage with her would spoil his prospects of a successful career, but she never ceased to love him, and refused to marry Charles Musgrove and later Mr Elliot because of him. She was prepared to accept her lot as the unwanted female, no enviable position in those days, rather than take the second best, and the reader feels a great satisfaction when her unselfishness and devotion are at last rewarded with happiness.

Captain Wentworth

A remarkably fine young man.

This is Jane Austen's description of the captain at the time when he first became engaged to Anne, and she follows it up by telling us that he had a 'great deal of intelligence, spirit, and brilliancy'.

The very fact that he had chosen to follow the sea as his career at a time when the risks of war made its dangers greater than normal shows that he was adventurous and brave; he could have no illusions about the life he had chosen, since Admiral Croft, his brother-in-law, could enlighten him. Like many sailors he was somewhat careless about money, spending freely when he came ashore and taking little heed for the future. It is his optimistic outlook which makes him behave like this, of course, and this again is typical of many of his profession, for Jane Austen, whose brothers were in the Navy, knew the type well and may, indeed, have been drawing the character from life.

When he reappears at Uppercross, Anne feels that the years have improved him physically and that he has 'a more glowing, manly, open look'. His character, too, has matured, although he is still somewhat over-confident, and heedless. His first careless remark, caused by the very real shock of seeing the change that seven years has made in Anne is very cruel; and although he did not intend it for her ears, a few minutes' thought would have shown him that it would most probably reach them. He had been very much in love with Anne in his younger days and therefore found it hard to forgive her treatment of him, which he ascribed to 'weakness and timidity'; yet in spite of himself he has remained loyal to her memory, and although he believes that her 'power with him was gone forever', it is his memory of Anne that he describes to his sister when he tells her of the qualities he wishes to find in his future wife. His luck has held throughout the war, and now that he is rich, he feels that it is time he found a wife and has come ashore with the intention of falling in love. Of course Henrietta and Louisa Musgrove attract him; they have the youth and gaiety which he had found in Anne seven years before, but he clearly sees their lack of intelligence and it is only a passing fancy. Henrietta's affections are already fixed on her cousin, Charles Hayter, and although Captain Wentworth seems genuinely impressed by what he believes to be Louisa's strength of character – he praises this when Anne overhears him on the autumn walk – he is never in love with her, and when she turns to Captain Benwick during her convalescence, he is very relieved since he had discovered that the Harvilles imagined him to be almost engaged to her.

Captain Wentworth is, of course, invariably considerate of all women; he dislikes the idea of their travelling on his ship because of the discomforts they must suffer; he listens without impatience to Mrs Musgrove's theories about her dead son; and it is he who makes sure that Anne gets a lift in his sister's carriage after her long walk, and indirectly sends her news from Lyme about the invalid. It is this same consideration which deceives Anne about his affection for Louisa when he remains in Lyme after the accident. By this time, however, he has recognized the true nature of his feeling for Anne, spurred on, of course, by the knowledge that Charles Musgrove had proposed to her before he married Mary, and that Mr Elliot also admired her. He begins, perhaps for the first time, to understand Anne's character fully, and at last knows that it is his own pride which has kept them apart so long, for she admits that if he had proposed to her again when he came ashore two years after his first proposal, she would gladly have accepted him. However, considering all things, we feel that he merits his good fortune in marrying Anne, and that he will not be 'happier than he deserves'.

Sir Walter Elliot

Vanity was the beginning and end of Sir Walter's character.

By the time Jane Austen came to write *Persuasion* she had learned to make every part of a novel subordinate to the whole, so that Sir Walter Elliot does not stand out among the other people in the book as Mr Collins does in *Pride and Prejudice.* In spite of this, however, he is one of the great comic characters of the novels, a man who is vain – as distinct from being proud – of his heritage, his looks and his position in society. He is vain of his heritage because he glories in the fact that he is a baronet and can, therefore, take precedence over those of lower rank, and not because he has any real pride in the achievements of his ancestors. He is vain of his looks, and when Admiral Croft rents Kellynch, he is amazed at the number of mirrors in Sir Walter's room and finds it necessary to remove most of them. When he is discussing the merits or demerits of a naval officer as a prospective tenant, he shows how vain he is of his looks, for he speaks with something approaching horror of the effects of a hard life at sea on the appearance. The fact that these naval officers have been engaged in a life and death struggle for the safety of England has, of course, never occurred to him, although when Anne reminds him of the value of the Navy, he admits that 'the profession has its utility'. On the same occasion he shows his vanity concerning his position in society, when he declares that 'a man is in greater danger in the Navy of being insulted by the rise of one whose father his father might have disdained to speak to . . . than in any other line'.

Like all men of his kind he can be easily persuaded by anyone who is prepared to flatter him, hence Mr Shepherd and Mrs Clay find him an easy victim although at times he can be obstinate. And as he likes people to flatter him, so he, in his turn, is ready to be obsequious to those of higher rank, and his behaviour to the Dowager-Viscountess Dalrymple and her daughter shows him at his worst.

His shallow nature makes him quite incapable of any strong human emotion, and Fate played a knavish trick on him when he was left with the responsibility of bringing up three young daughters. It was indeed fortunate that Lady Russell was at hand to take an interest in them, for their father cared only for their looks, about which his comments were tactless and outspoken. At Bath he told Anne that he 'would send Mary a new hat and pelisse' – and how Mary would have valued this attention from her father – 'if it would not tempt her to go out in sharp winds and grow coarse'. Elizabeth is, naturally, his favourite, for she is handsome and shares her father's ideas, and for this reason he is really fond of her.

He judges everyone by appearances; he approves of Captain Wentworth, when he meets him at Bath, because he is a 'very well-looking man', and condemns his heir for being 'very much under-hung'; he recommends that Mrs Clay should use Gowland for her freckles, and is disturbed at the increase of crow's feet around Lady Russell's temples. Indeed he has gained no store of wisdom with the passing of the years, and shows that he is as foolish in middle age as he could ever have been in youth.

Elizabeth

She was fully satisfied of being still quite as handsome as ever, but she felt her approach to the years of danger.

Elizabeth, the eldest daughter of Sir Walter Elliot, is the one most like her father. This is not surprising, as she has been his close companion since the death of her mother when she was sixteen. True, she is not quite as self-satisfied as he, for at the age of twenty-nine she is still unmarried. As a young girl she had made up her mind to marry Mr Walter Elliot, her father's heir and the only man, in her estimation, equal in rank to herself. Of course the advantages of such a marriage were enormous, for she would become Lady Elliot at her father's death and live at her old home. Mr Elliot was at that time a law student, and she was able to see him when she spent a season in Town. But the scheme had fallen through, since Mr Elliot, although apparently pleased to see her in London, had been unwilling to visit her in the country and had soon married 'a rich woman of inferior birth'. When he reappears as an eligible widower, Elizabeth is quite prepared to smile upon him again.

In spite of this willingness to overlook her earlier humiliation, Elizabeth is as proud of her rank as her father, although she does not read *The Baronetage* so frequently as in her early days, since it reminds her that she has not yet made the great marriage which she had once so confidently expected. Her pride is, perhaps, a little less ridiculous than that of Mary, since her position is more secure and for thirteen years she had taken precedence of every other lady in the neighbourhood, except Lady Russell, in leaving the dining room after dinner. Like her father she is a snob, only too willing to make much of her aristocratic relatives, the Dowager-Viscountess Dalrymple and her daughter, the Honourable Miss Carteret; like him, too, she talks glibly of 'our cousins', taking care to let everyone hear about her important connections. Jane Austen gives an amusing example of this when she describes the scene as the two sisters and Mrs Clay are sheltering from the rain at Molland's in Milsom Street. 'There was a delay, and a bustle, and a talking, which must make all the little crowd in the shop understand that Lady Dalrymple was calling to convey Miss Elliot.' Her snobbish attitude is also seen in her behaviour to Captain Wentworth; when she first meets him in Bath, she refuses to know him, but later, after Lady Dalrymple's remarks about his distinguished air, she is quite gracious towards him.

Her own regard for rank and wealth makes her appreciate a similar regard in others – 'To flatter and follow others without being flattered and followed in turn is but a state of half-enjoyment.' – and Mrs Clay finds her an easy dupe. Money is short, Kellynch Hall must be handed over to a tenant, and yet Elizabeth finds it necessary to take this scheming woman to Bath.

Vain and self-centred, she has, of course, none of Anne's consideration for other people, and looks at everything from her own point of view. When her father broke the news to her that his income was dwindling steadily and warned her that something must be done, her first ideas of economizing were 'to cut off some unnecessary charities', and 'to take no present down to Anne' when they returned from their season in Town. True she also decided not to refurnish the drawing-room, but one feels that since she felt herself ill-used by the turn of events, she probably lamented this as a great sacrifice on her part.

When the story ends, one is left with a feeling of pity for Elizabeth, growing more and more discontented with her lot, and having had 'the mortification of seeing Mr Elliot withdraw, and no one of proper condition has since presented himself to raise even the unfounded hopes which sunk with him'.

Mary Musgrove

Inheriting a considerable share of the Elliot self-importance.

Mary, the youngest daughter of Sir Walter, has much in common with her father and eldest sister. She shares their snobbish attitude and their pride, but whereas they have the dignity and self-assurance to make most people accept them at their face value and do as they wish, no one takes much notice of Mary and she has to insist upon her rights and privileges. When she dined with her husband's parents she was constantly annoyed, for Mrs Musgrove often forgot to arrange that she should take precedence of the ladies of lower rank. At Lyme, too, her vanity is wounded at first by Mrs Harville, who gives her mother-in-law the place to which she, Mary, is entitled because of her higher rank; when Mrs Harville discovers her mistake and apologizes, Mary begins to enjoy herself again.

According to Mrs Musgrove she spoils her children thoroughly, probably because she has not enough real interest in them to take any trouble in training them, and when the eldest boy dislocates his collar-bone, she shows no thought for him but merely becomes hysterical, and on the next day insists upon accompanying her husband to the Great House for dinner. The arguments with which, on this occasion, she seeks to convince Anne that a mother is not the best person to be with a sick child show her shallow nature at its worst. Of course she is of no use in an emergency, and only adds to the confusion at Lyme when Louisa's accident occurs.

Jane Austen tells us, with great irony, that Mary's father has had little regard for her at any time, and this probably accounts for much of her craving for attention. She was the third girl to be born in the family when her father wanted an heir, and although she had acquired 'a little artificial importance in becoming Mrs Charles Musgrove', this did not last long. It was common knowledge in the family, too, that Charles had first proposed to Anne and been rejected by her, a fact which Mary's vanity may have found difficult to accept. Her husband's family found her trying at times and one can sympathize with Louisa when she expresses her opinion of her sister-in-law to Captain Wentworth: 'Mary is good-natured enough in many respects, but she does sometimes provoke me by her nonsense and pride – the Elliot pride . . . we do so wish that Charles had married Anne instead.'

She is as selfish as Elizabeth but, again, she has not the ability to make herself the centre of attraction. She becomes petulant when she is left alone, and imagines herself to be ill and neglected. Anne finds her in this mood when she first arrives at Uppercross, but a little sympathy soon restores her to her usual frame of mind. She shows no consideration for Anne, of course, and tactlessly repeats to her Captain Wentworth's remark that she was so altered that he would not have known her again.

Perhaps her character is best shown in her letter. Her complaints about the dullness of life in the country, about Mrs Musgrove's liking for the Harville children, about Mrs Clay's long stay at Bath, and about her own ailments; her fickle change of attitude towards the Crofts, her sneers about Henrietta's forthcoming marriage, her surprise at Louisa's engagement to Captain Benwick and her tactless remark: 'And this is the end, you see, of Captain Benwick's being supposed to be an admirer of yours'; all these reveal her as the sister 'who was not so repulsive and unsisterly as Elizabeth, nor so inaccessible to all influence', perhaps, but they do show her as a most unpleasant person.

Lady Russell

Of steady age and character.

When Lady Elliot died leaving three young daughters, it was

Lady Russell who acted as their friend and adviser. She had loved their mother, who must have found her invaluable as a confidante when life with Sir Walter became too difficult. Anne, her god-daughter, was her favourite among the three girls since she was the most like her mother, and it was Anne who stayed with her for long periods at a time.

Although she is not quick-witted, her judgment is sound and she has also a great sense of honour; it is for these reasons that everyone consults her when in difficulty. Mr Shepherd thinks of her at once when he wishes to persuade Sir Walter to let Kellynch, and Anne trusted her so much in her youth, and had always found her so anxious for her happiness, that she broke off her engagement to Frederick Wentworth because Lady Russell declared it to be indiscreet, although, of course, Anne's motive was not mere caution but a belief that the engagement might harm her lover's future prospects.

Lady Russell is set in her ideas and habits at the time when the story begins, and she has nothing in common with the Musgrove and Harville children who are staying at Uppercross for Christmas and finds the noise they make intolerable. Her preference for the winter is a settled, ordered life at Bath, spent in calling on her friends and going to concerts and the theatre.

She has a cultivated mind and is very sensible about most things, but she has a weakness for rank, and is prepared to forgive Sir Walter a great deal since he is a baronet, while she is only the widow of a knight. Although she is able to see through the designs of Mrs Clay, who is of low birth, she is quite decieved by Mr Elliot, because of his prospects and because of her own pet schemes. She would like to see Anne marry her father's heir and so take her mother's place at Kellynch later on. When at last she is made to understand what kind of a man he is – and the discovery is a shock and gives her great pain, for he is the heir to a baronetcy – she is good-natured enough to admit her mistake and then sets out to make other plans.

Mrs Clay

One artful woman.

When Lady Russell first heard of the suggestion that Sir Walter Elliot's family should leave Kellynch and settle in Bath, she was very pleased, because this, she thought, would mean that Elizabeth would be separated from Mrs Clay, of whom Lady Russell thoroughly disapproved since she believed that the woman was clever enough to use Elizabeth's friendship for her own purposes. When we first meet Mrs Clay, we realize at once how true is Lady Russell's judgment. On this occasion the schemer has come to Kellynch with her father, Mr Shepherd, because, as Jane Austen tells us, with malicious humour, 'nothing was of so much use to Mrs Clay's health as a drive to Kellynch'.

There is no doubt that she has summed up the characters of Sir Walter and Elizabeth with accuracy and knows exactly how to bring them round to her point of view. She uses just the right arguments to convince Sir Walter that a naval officer would be an ideal tenant, and when he launches into an account of the ageing effect of a life at sea, with anecdotes about various officers of his acquaintance, she brings him back to the point while cleverly flattering him. Her fluent speech is reminiscent of her father's, whom she probably imitates, perhaps unconsciously.

It is quite possible that she plans to marry Sir Walter, but she knows that if Elizabeth suspected this, she would never be allowed in his company, and so she pretends to be the humble but helpful friend, so ugly, with her projecting tooth and her freckles, that no one could possibly think her dangerous. Anne, of course, is as suspicious of her as Lady Russell when she finds that Elizabeth is actually proposing to take Mrs Clay to Bath, but her protests are disregarded, and Elizabeth shows the impression which has been skilfully planted in her mind, 'Poor Mrs Clay, who with all her merits can never have been reckoned tolerably pretty, I really think poor Mrs Clay may be staying here in perfect safety.'

It is significant of the progress of Mrs Clay's scheme that when Anne arrives at Bath, and her father compliments her on her improved complexion, he adds, 'I should recommend Gowland . . . during the spring months. Mrs Clay has been using it at my recommendation, and you see what it has done for her. You see how it has carried away her freckles.'

When Mr Elliot becomes a visitor at Camden Place, he has already heard about the danger of a possible marriage between

Mrs Clay and Sir Walter, and as this might deprive him of the title, he has determined to prevent it. His method is, of course, to pretend to admire her himself, and we have the amusing spectacle of these two hypocrites indulging in a battle of wits. On one occasion Mrs Clay is almost found out, but when Anne deliberately mentions that she has been seen talking to Mr Elliot when he is supposed to have left Bath, her quick brain and glib tongue get her swiftly out of the difficulty. When at last Anne is to marry Captain Wentworth, and Mr Elliot leaves Bath since he has no further hopes at the moment, he takes Mrs Clay away also. 'Mrs Clay's affections had over-powered her interest,' as Jane Austen tells us, 'and she had sacrificed for the young man's sake, the possibility of scheming longer for Sir Walter.'

But this is not the end of the story, for their battle of wits continued and it was not clear which would win. Perhaps in the end Mrs Clay was more than a match for Sir Walter's heir, and 'after preventing her from being the wife of Sir Walter', he might 'be wheedled and caressed at last into making her the wife of Sir William'.

Mr Elliot

A man without heart or conscience.

In her younger days Elizabeth Elliot had fixed her hopes on a marriage with her cousin without knowing anything of his character. At the time he was a poor law student whose one idea was to get a fortune as quickly as possible and by any means, fair or foul. Elizabeth had little money and therefore he was not attracted. The baronetcy which he might one day inherit meant nothing to him – indeed Mrs Smith says she had heard him frequently declare that 'if baronetcies were saleable, anyone should have his for fifty pounds, arms and motto, name and livery included'. Perhaps it seemed at that time a remote possibility that he would ever inherit, for Sir Walter was a comparatively young man and likely to marry again. It was at this time that he wrote the letter to Mr Smith in which he showed his true opinion of his relatives at Kellynch. 'I have got rid of Sir Walter and Miss . . . The baronet . . . is worse than last year.'

His quest for an easy fortune led him to marry a woman of low rank, a grazier's daughter. Again we are indebted to Mrs Smith for an account of the marriage and of the callous way in which he behaved. Apparently his wife was a woman of good education who fell genuinely in love with him, but he made sure of the amount of her fortune before he married her. As a result of this marriage he became very wealthy, but he felt no gratitude towards the friends who had formerly helped him; indeed he seems to have deliberately encouraged Charles Smith to ruin himself. When the crash came and the widow was left to deal with her husband's financial difficulties, she found that Mr Elliot even refused to act as executor under Mr Smith's will, and showed ingratitude amounting to inhumanity. There was certain property in the West Indies which could have yielded a good income, if Mr Elliot had bothered to deal with the legal troubles, but even this he refused to do.

Like many wealthy people who have once been poor, he has become cautious in money matters, when he appears in the story, and now begins to value his chance of inheriting a title and estates. He is warned by his friend, Colonel Wallis, that 'a clever, insinuating, handsome woman, poor and plausible', is doing her best to persuade Sir Walter into marriage, so he comes to Bath to keep watch and succeeds in getting Mrs Clay to transfer her attentions to himself. His wife is dead and he is considering a second marriage. When he saw Anne at Lyme he really admired her, and on learning who she is, determines that she shall be his wife. He is clever enough to make himself acceptable to his cousins, even giving Elizabeth the impression that he may propose to her, and his insincerity rivals that of Mrs Clay. When Anne's engagement is announced, he realizes that his plans have failed; there is one thing he can do, however, and that, of course, is to persuade Mrs Clay to leave Bath so that the baronet is preserved from marriage with her, but whether this scheme is really to his advantage, we do not know.

Mr and Mrs Musgrove

A very good sort of people.

Mr and Mrs Musgrove are an old-fashioned couple with a large family, a beautiful estate and an adequate income. They are happy and homely people who find their pleasure in caring for their children, and they have little desire to follow the whims of the fashionable world. They are indulgent parents who, when their eldest son marries, provide him with an attractive house, and when their daughters return from boarding-school with new ideas, allow them to give the old-fashioned parlour 'the proper air of confusion by a grand pianoforte and a harp, flower-stands and little tables placed in every direction'. They are hospitable and friendly and are only too glad to be able to repay the Harvilles for their kindness to Louisa by having their children to stay at Uppercross. The scene there on the afternoon when Lady Russell and Anne paid their last call before going to Bath was one of confusion but happiness. They are not well educated, and Anne decides that although she envies them their mutual understanding and affection, she 'would not have given up her own more elegant and cultivated mind for all their enjoyment'.

Mr Musgrove is the typical country squire of the eighteenth century, occupying his time with his dogs and his horses, taking an interest in all the affairs of his family, and showing himself to be very stolid and reliable in times of trouble.

Mrs Musgrove's kindliness and good humour are shown on every occasion. She compliments Anne on her playing when the young people are dancing at Uppercross; she overwhelms her and the Harvilles with thanks for caring for Louisa, and has a good word to say about everyone. There was one great sorrow in her life, the death of her son, Richard, who had been a ne'er-do-well and had been sent to sea where he served under Captain Wentworth. His mother has forgotten his faults, however, and laments a promising life cut off at its beginning. When she sees Captain Wentworth she declares: 'If it had pleased Heaven to spare my poor son, I dare say he would have been just such another by this time.'

She is not in the least snobbish and although she would have liked Henrietta to marry someone with more money than Charles Hayter, she consoles herself with the thought that they are very much in love, and sensibly rejoices that they need not have a long engagement.

In spite of her good qualities, however, Mrs Musgrove is stupid in many ways and her conversation boring to those who have to listen to it. She has only one idea in her mind at a time and this she works to death. When Anne first comes to Uppercross it is Mary's lack of control over her children: 'You know it is bad to have children with one that one is obliged to be checking every moment, "don't do this", and "don't do that"; or that one can only keep in tolerable order by more cake than is good for them.' When Captain Wentworth visits her, it is her son's career in the Navy, and when Mrs Croft calls upon her at the White Hart in Bath, it is Henrietta's approaching marriage which she discusses with 'minutiae which, even with every advantage of taste and delicacy . . . could be properly interesting only to the principals'. Anne hoped, on that occasion 'that the gentlemen might be too much self-occupied to hear'.

Henrietta and Louisa Musgrove

And very nice young ladies they both are; I hardly know one from the other.

Admiral Croft's judgment upon the Musgrove girls is, apparently, true at the beginning of the novel. When we first meet them at Uppercross they have only recently returned from the boarding-school at Exeter where they have learned to play the pianoforte and the harp, and to be fashionable. They are full of high spirits and youthful gaiety, good-tempered, and mad for dancing and pleasure, with little to distinguish them from each other. They utter a great deal of inconsequential chatter, and even the accident to their nephew, young Charles, cannot subdue them for long. Of course, they are excited when Captain Wentworth comes to visit them, for they find him more handsome and experienced than any of the men they know and are as eager as their mother to look up the Navy List for details of his career.

It is on the autumn walk that we first see that the sisters have a stronger and more serious side to their natures. Henrietta is really in love with her cousin, Charles Hayter, the curate, but she is at the same time attracted by Frederick Wentworth, so that she is in danger of throwing away the substance for the shadow. Persuaded by her sister, she now decides to call at Winthrop, the Hayters' home, and see Charles. She needs Louisa's support, however, to withstand Mary's snobbish remarks, so it seems that Louisa is the stronger of the two. At the time of the accident, however, Anne wonders how much of Louisa's apparent strength of character, so much praised by Captain Wentworth, is merely obstinacy, for had she not persisted in jumping from the steps against the captain's advice she would not have been hurt.

During this walk it is also revealed that the two girls are shrewdly conscious of the absurdity of Mary's pride and insistence upon rank, and that they have not much opinion of their sister-in-law, to whom they would have preferred Anne.

At Lyme they are again the thoughtless young ladies, praising the scenery, the Navy and everything else with which they come in contact. Henrietta's simplicity is such that we see quite clearly what she is thinking, when she declares how much good the sea air would do to Dr Shirley, the elderly Vicar of Uppercross, and his wife, and protests against his being forced to remain at his Vicarage, when he might live at Lyme and have his work done, as Anne points out, 'by some active, respectable young man as a resident curate'.

Obviously the sisters are deeply attached to each other, for after the accident to Louisa, Henrietta faints and is most distressed, and later, on the journey to Uppercross, she cries herself to sleep. This unfortunate event seems to make both sisters grow up; Henrietta's wish that Charles Hayter should find a living is fulfilled and she devotes her time to preparations for her marriage, while Louisa's long convalescence makes her more serious and mature also, so that she is attracted by Captain Benwick and agrees to marry him.

Charles Musgrove

Civil and agreeable.

If Anne had married Charles Musgrove he might have become more mature and serious-minded. As it is, with Mary as his wife, he has no one to encourage him to be interested in books and he is enthusiastic only about sport; indeed, he judges everyone by an interest in sport and has a greater respect for Captain Benwick after they have been rat-hunting together. He is good-tempered and generous, bearing no ill will when, as sometimes happens, his father does not give him a money present he is expecting. He will even tell the resentful Mary, on such occasions, that his father has 'many other uses for his money, and a right to spend it as he likes'. He suffers his wife's fits of depression with few complaints, although he does at times express a wish that she would not always fancy herself to be ill, and deals with her unreasonable ideas so firmly and patiently that he wins Anne's admiration. He is fond of his children and manages them much better than his wife can do; when they are ill he is distressed, but as soon as they show signs of recovery, he quickly reverts to his normal way of life. He is also fond of his mother and sisters; he refuses to leave Louisa after the accident, declaring that he 'neither ought nor would' leave her in such a state. Later on, in Bath, he seems genuinely anxious to please Mrs Musgrove and takes a box for her at the theatre. There is a very boyish side to his character which comes out in the scene when he returns to the hotel after booking the box. He makes a face behind the backs of Sir Walter and Elizabeth when he has bowed them out of the room, and then teases his wife by declaring that he has no desire to meet her father's heir, and would rather go to the theatre than to the evening party, which is probably true. Altogether he is a pleasant person who makes the best of most situations, and if Mary is not an ideal wife for him, at least, as Jane Austen tells us, 'they might pass for a happy couple. They were always perfectly agreed in the want of more money and a strong inclination for a handsome present from his father' (VI).

Admiral and Mrs Croft

Such a pleasant family.

The Crofts are as happily married as the Musgroves but the circumstances of their lives have been very different, and it is doubtful whether Mrs Musgrove would have shared hardships with her husband as Mrs Croft has done. When they first come to Kellynch and so into the story, the admiral has achieved a good position and a handsome fortune by his service at sea. He has been with Nelson at Trafalgar and afterwards has been stationed in the West Indies; now he wants a comfortable home where he can settle down as a country gentleman, and, in order to get it, is prepared to pay more or less what is asked. Mr Shepherd describes him as 'a very hale, hearty, well-looking man, a little weather-beaten, to be sure, but not much, and quite the gentleman in all his motions and behaviour' (III). He is simple in his tastes and modest about his own appearance, so that he finds Sir Walter's collection of mirrors most embarrassing. His manners are bluff and hearty, and when Anne and Lady Russell call upon him and his wife, Anne is afraid that they 'were not quite of the tone to suit Lady Russell', although she herself is delighted with his simplicity. Later, when Louisa becomes engaged to Benwick, he comments to her, about his brother-in-law's letter, that there is nothing in it to cause uneasiness about his feelings 'for there is not an oath or a murmur from beginning to end'. He is both good-humoured and good-hearted, and shows consideration for all the people with whom he comes into contact. He is most distressed lest he should hurt Anne's feelings at her old home, and gives her permission to go where she wishes. When she meets him in Bath, his pleasure that she has spoken to him and his out-spoken comments on the print of a boat in a shop window are delightful. He is, of course, devoted to his wife and loves to point out how little time elapsed between their first meeting and their 'sitting down together' in their lodgings at North Yarmouth.

Mrs Croft is described by Mr Shepherd as a 'very well-spoken genteel, shrewd lady'. She it is who asks questions about the rent and taxes of Kellynch and investigates all the details which her husband neglects. The way in which they drive the gig, to Anne's amusement, on her return from the autumn walk is a good illustration of their relations in life. The admiral actually drives, but when he is in danger of running into a post or a rut, his wife takes a hand, and 'by coolly giving the reins a better direction herself, they happily pass the danger'. She is a sensible, level-headed woman who makes friends easily with Lady Russell and listens with tolerance to Mrs Musgrove. Her affection for her husband is as strong as his affection for her; she has shared the hardships of a life at sea for fifteen years and sacrificed her youth and looks in doing so. When Anne first meets her at Mary's house, she notices that 'she had bright dark eyes, good teeth and altogether an agreeable face; though her reddened and weatherbeaten complexion, the consequence of her having been almost as much at sea as her husband, made her seem to have lived some years longer in the world than her real eight-

and-thirty' (VI). She is full of praise for conditions on board ship, however, declaring that the five in which she has lived have afforded her comforts equal to those at Kellynch Hall. She frankly admits to having always been sea-sick during her first twenty-four hours on board, but says that after that she was thoroughly happy. All this seems to show that she had plenty of courage. Even the thought of danger from ship-wreck or from the enemy did not daunt her as long as she was with her husband; when he left her on shore, however, her anxiety was so great that she was miserable and spent her time imagining the accidents that might befall him.

Captain Benwick

An excellent, good-hearted fellow . . . rather too piano.

Anne and the other members of the party from Uppercross are very favourably disposed towards Captain Benwick before they meet him, since Captain Wentworth has told them about the death of his fiancée, Fanny Harville, while he was at sea. Wentworth explains that Benwick is a man 'uniting very strong feelings with quiet, serious and retiring manners, and a decided taste for reading and sedentary pursuits'. When they actually see him, his melancholy air and lack of conversation increase their sympathy towards him. Next day Anne is thrown by chance into his company again and she finds that though he is shy, he is very friendly and eager to talk to anyone who shares his tastes. The poets whose works appeal to him are Sir Walter Scott and Byron, and it is the romantic passages concerning broken hearts and great wretchedness which he has taken the trouble to commit to memory. Anne feels that this attitude towards his sorrow is unhealthy and recommends that he should read more prose, essays and memoirs, which would give him a sterner view of life and show him how people have faced great grief and overcome it. He accepts her recommendation but shows quite plainly that he does not think it will succeed. His eagerness to talk to Anne, which to Mary means that he must be her admirer, really shows that he is craving for womanly understanding and is, therefore, ready to be interested in any woman who will supply it. This is emphasized when Charles invites him to Uppercross, and, when he finds that Anne is staying some considerable distance away, he refuses the invitation at the last moment. When Louisa's accident occurs and he is thrown into her company day after day, the result is inevitable, and perhaps only Captain Harville, who regards this new attachment as something of a slight to his sister's memory, is really surprised. From what we see of Captain Benwick during these incidents in the book, we might not have a great opinion of him as a naval officer but he is resourceful in the emergency on the Cobb and we have an assurance from Admiral Croft that he is 'a very active, zealous officer'. Charles Musgrove, too, discovers to his surprise that Benwick's 'reading has done him no harm', and tells Anne, 'He is a brave fellow. I got more acquainted with him last Monday than ever I did before. We had a famous set-to at rat-hunting all the morning in my father's great barns; and he played his part so well that I have liked him the better ever since' (XXII).

Mrs Smith

Good sense and agreeable manners.

The part played in the story by Mrs Smith is an important one, although she does not appear until the second half of the book. Anne remembers with gratitude her kindness at school when, as a girl of seventeen, she befriended the fourteen-year-old Anne who had been sent away from home on the death of her mother. When they next meet, the positions are reversed; Mrs Smith is now a widow, living in poverty and constant suffering, and glad to see again 'the elegant little woman of seven-and-twenty', who spares time from the fashionable world to come and visit her. The qualities in Mrs Smith's character which impress Anne at this meeting, after twelve years, are her cheerfulness and her interest in the people around her. Although she is condemned to live in two small and noisy rooms and to depend upon the help of the busy servant of the lodging-house when she wishes to move from one to the other, she has only moments of depression. Her troubles have taught her that the one way to overcome self-pity is to keep busy at some kind of work, preferably work for others. So, crippled and poor as she is, she spends her time making 'thread-cases, pin-cushions and card-racks' which Nurse Rooke sells for her and which provide her with the money to help those who are poorer than herself. She even disdains the name of invalid and insists that, although it might have been applicable to her in the dreary days when she first arrived in Bath, she has now discarded it. Debarred as she is both by sickness and poverty from entering the fashionable world, she still remembers her earlier days with delight, and is woman enough to listen eagerly to the gossip which is brought to her by Nurse Rooke. She knows all about Mr Elliot's plans to marry Anne, and to prevent the marriage of Sir Walter and Mrs Clay long before Anne herself realizes them. She understands the true nature of Sir Walter's heir and feels a natural bitterness towards him because of his share in her husband's ruin, and his refusal to get her rights, yet she is sufficiently a woman of the world to mask her true feelings and to show pleasure in the probability, as she believes, of Anne's marriage to him. She even praises him, and without hypocrisy, for she is careful to choose the qualities in him which merit praise. Nor is she unkind to Anne in congratulating her on having gained the attentions of a man whom she knows to be cruel and worthless, for she believes that the matter has already been arranged, and that to enlighten Anne could only hurt her without doing any good. She also knows that Mr Elliot will never behave towards Anne as he did towards his first wife. In showing Mrs Smith's ways of getting information and the rumours which circulate in Bath, Jane Austen is satirizing the gossips and showing how far from the truth they often are.

Style

In one of her letters which has been preserved, Jane Austen wrote, 'An artist cannot do anything slovenly,' and this statement reveals to us her aim in every novel she produced. Precision, simplicity, accuracy, these are the qualities she valued and these are the qualities we find in her writings. Perhaps it was her close study of the writers of the eighteenth century and her admiration for them, especially for Dr Johnson, which influenced her towards that clarity which so many people have remarked upon, for the eighteenth century demanded lucidity from a writer above all things; Dr Johnson himself wrote, 'Proper words in proper places make the true definition of a style.'

When she first began to write she chose the shorter simple sentences or compound ones on very many occasions, and seemed almost to distrust any elaboration of sentence structure, for example, in *Pride and Prejudice*, Miss Bingley sums up the accomplishments necessary to a woman of her class thus: 'A woman must have a thorough knowledge of music, singing, drawing, dancing and the modern languages to deserve the word; and besides all this, she must possess a certain something in her air and manner of walking.' There are, of course, innumerable examples of a similar kind. As she became more skilled in her technique, however, she seems to have realized that it is possible to weave words into complicated sentences and yet to retain clarity and accuracy, for example, 'It succeeded, however; and though Sir Walter must ever look with an evil eye on anyone intending to inhabit that house, and think them infinitely too well off in being permitted to rent it on the highest terms, he was talked into allowing Mr Shepherd to proceed in the treaty and authorising him to wait on Admiral Croft, who still remained at Taunton and fix a day for the house being seen.' Here we have a long and elaborate sentence which is not only perfectly clear, but at the same time suggests the long-winded, tortuous reasoning of Mr Shepherd's legal mind.

Like that of all good writers her style developed, and since *Persuasion* is one of the novels for which the manuscript of part of a first draft exists, it is possible to see how carefully she changed and corrected her work. It was, as we have said, one of the later novels, and by the time she wrote or revised it, she had learned perfectly how to vary the pace of a narrative, when to use conversation and when to report what was said, and above all, how to convey every subtle trait of character and shade of meaning in a conversation. Among the finest things she ever did – and from the first she was a brilliant writer of dialogue – is the account of Anne's visit to the Musgrove party at the White Hart hotel (XXIII). When she arrived, Mrs Musgrove was giving Mrs Croft the history of her daughter's engagement, and 'just in that inconvenient tone of voice which was perfectly audible while it pretended to be a whisper'. Nothing could be more natural, each one of us has surely listened to such a conversation at some time or other, with the chattering of silly Mrs

Musgrove about 'what my brother Hayter had said one day, and what Mr Musgrove had proposed the next, and what had occurred to my sister Hayter' . . . etc., contrasted with the matter-of-fact statements of practical Mrs Croft: 'I would rather have young people settle on a small income at once,' and so on. While these ladies continue their talk, Anne is taken apart by Captain Harville, and another conversation ensues, a conversation which contrasts in every way with that we have just heard. Both Anne and Captain Harville are deeply moved at this time; Anne by the somewhat unexpected presence of Captain Wentworth and Captain Harville by the thought of his dead sister, since he has been commissioned by Captain Benwick to arrange for the miniature intended for Miss Harville to be reset for Louisa Musgrove, and the tension in their minds shows itself in their conversation. 'Poor Fanny! she would not have forgotten him so soon,' says Captain Harville, and Anne uses this statement to declare the loyalty of her own sex. 'We certainly do not forget you so soon as you forget us. It is, perhaps, our fate rather than our merit, we cannot help ourselves. We live at home, quiet, confined, and our feelings prey upon us. You are forced on exertion. You have always a profession, pursuits, business of some sort or other . . .' It is a dramatic moment for the reader, who knows that although Anne is speaking to one man, she is actually addressing the other one who sits quietly by, apparently intent on his letter. This is a magnificent piece of dialogue and could be used on the stage with little, if any, alteration.

In *Persuasion* Jane Austen reports more conversations than in the early books, for she seems to have discovered that, quite frequently, no good purpose is served by giving the actual words spoken when the speakers are sensible people conversing on trivial topics. Thus when Lady Russell pays her courtesy call on Mrs Croft at Kellynch Hall, their conversation is indirectly recorded: 'The sad accident at Lyme was soon the prevailing topic, and on comparing their latest accounts of the invalid, it appeared that each lady dated her intelligence from the same hour of yestermorn . . .' (XIII). When she is dealing with characters like Mrs Musgrove or May, who are not sensible, or with those like Admiral Croft, who have strong individuality, even eccentricity, direct speech is almost always used, and the character becomes more and more real to us because of it. How much we learn about Admiral Croft when he talks to Anne about her father: 'I should think he must be rather a dressy man for his time of life. Such a number of looking-glasses! Oh, Lord! there was no getting away from one's self. So I got Sophy to lend me a hand, and we soon shifted their quarters; and now I am quite snug, with my little shaving-glass in one corner, and another great thing that I never go near' (XIII).

There is a distinct nautical flavour to everything the Admiral says, and yet, like all Jane Austen's sailors, including Captains Wentworth, Benwick and Harville, he uses no exaggerated expressions; his speech rings true, and one can imagine that it was modelled on the language of Frank and Charles, Jane's two sailor brothers, and their friends.

The speech of Mrs Clay, the lawyer's daughter whose ambition to become Lady Elliot worries Lady Russell and Anne, is very brilliantly planned to suggest not only her lower social rank but also her insincerity. She not only uses unsuitable words but attempts long, involved sentences which she finds herself unable to complete. When she is helping her father to persuade Sir Walter to let Kellynch to Admiral Croft, she points out that all professions have an adverse effect on the looks of those who follow them: 'The lawyer plods, quite care-worn; the physician is up at all hours, and travelling in all weathers; and even the clergyman? . . . she stopt a moment to consider what might do for the clergyman – "and even the clergyman, you know, is obliged to go into infected rooms" ' (III). We feel that her manner of conversation is based on something she has heard or read and imperfectly remembered.

Jane Austen's wit is shown both in narrative and in conversation. When Sir Walter and Elizabeth leave their home, she tells us in the narration, with biting sarcasm, that Sir Walter was 'prepared with condescending bows for all the afflicted tenantry and cottagers who might have had a hint to shew themselves' (V); and when Admiral Croft speaks to Anne of the Musgrove girls he shows much unconscious wit.

Occasionally the style is more formal than the English to which we are accustomed today, partly because of the period in which she is writing, and partly because of her great admiration for Dr Johnson and the eighteenth-century essayists, which has already been mentioned. Of Anne's conversation with Captain Benwick at Lyme we are told, 'She thought it the misfortune of poetry to be seldom safely enjoyed by those who enjoyed it completely; and that the strong feelings which alone could estimate it truly were the very feelings which ought to taste it sparingly' (XI). The antithesis and the formality of this passage make it very much like a piece of eighteenth-century writing. The use of antithesis is, of course, frequent throughout the novel. Another good example occurs when we are told of Mrs Smith that 'Neither the dissipations of the past – and she had lived very much in the world – nor the restrictions of the present, neither sickness nor sorrow seemed to have closed her heart or ruined her spirits' (XVII).

We may also notice the skilful use of abstract expressions, for example, Sir Walter, Elizabeth and Mrs Clay step forward to meet Lady Dalrymple 'with all the eagerness compatible with anxious elegance'; and of similes – 'if he really sought to reconcile himself like a dutiful branch, he must be forgiven for having dismembered himself from the paternal tree.'

The style in the narrative parts of the novel is as effective as that in the passages of dialogue, for Jane Austen varies the general impression and atmosphere to suit the people and events she is writing about. One can hear Mrs Musgrove in the paragraph which describes Anne's attempts to get away from the White Hart after she has read Captain Wentworth's letter. 'The chair was earnestly protested against, and Mrs. Musgrove, who thought only of one sort of illness, having assured herself with some anxiety that there had been no fall in the case; that Anne had not at any time lately slipped down and got a blow on her head; that she was perfectly convinced of having had no fall, could part with her cheerfully, and depend on finding her better at night' (XXIII).

Equally skilful is the account of Anne's wait in the Cottage at Uppercross after Louisa's accident, with its subtle suggestion of mood and atmosphere. 'An hour's complete leisure for such reflexions as these, on a dark November day, a small thick rain almost blotting out the very few objects ever to be discerned from the window, was enough to make the sound of Lady Russell's carriage exceedingly welcome; and yet, though desirous to be gone, she could not quit the Mansion House, or look an adieu to the Cottage, with its black, dripping and comfortless verandah, or even notice through the misty glasses the last humble tenement of the village, without a saddened heart' (XIII).

Into each of her books Jane Austen has introduced one or more letters and *Persuasion* has three important ones. The first, that written by Mary to Anne, is typical of the writer and her attitude to life. She is as petulant in this as in her conversation and complains of the dullness of her life; mentions her husband's family disparagingly, and then, characteristically, gives her important news, of the engagement of Louisa and Captain Benwick, in a postscript. The second letter is the one sent by Mr Elliot to Charles Smith, and shown to Anne by Smith's widow. This is brutally curt in style and language; the sentences are simple or compound, and mostly short so as to give an almost staccato effect, and the whole reveals the unpleasant character of the writer. The third letter, from Captain Wentworth to Anne, is equally simple and abrupt, and from a similar cause. Captain Wentworth, like Mr Elliot, is moved by strong emotion, although whereas with Mr Elliot it is hatred and contempt for his cousins which makes him write in such a way, with Wentworth it is his faithful love for Anne which has roused him to plead his cause with her once more. Again brief disjointed sentences are used, with much repetition of short, decisive words and several rhetorical questions. In spite of the different style of this letter, however, he, too, puts the most important part of his appeal in the postscript.

It has sometimes been said that in Jane Austen's novels 'nothing ever happens', and critics have remarked that although she lived at a time when the whole of the continent of Europe was tormented by the Napoleonic Wars, and southern England feared a French invasion, her work gives no indication of the troubled times. There is a well-known story that Mr J. S. Clarke, the librarian to the Prince Regent, once tried to persuade her to write an historical novel, but that she refused since, as she wrote, 'I could no more write a romance than an epic poem, and if it were indispensable for me to keep it up and never relax into laughter at myself or other people, I am sure I should be hung before I had finished the first chapter.' She was very wise, for unlike many lesser writers, she recognized her own limitations and kept within them. Within her own kingdom, however, she is superb. She gives us such a clear and convincing picture of the life of Anne Elliot and her friends and relatives that we are able to enter a new world, gentler and more leisurely than our own. The events of the story may not be startling – a girl's fall on the steps of the Cobb and a visit to Bath – yet the effects of those events on the hearts and minds of the people concerned are as far-reaching as the most exciting adventure could be. There are moments that are tensely dramatic, and none the less effective for being related in a quiet, matter-of-fact way. Anne's dread of a meeting with Captain Wentworth is expressed again and again, but when at last it does occur, there is nothing to indicate the tumult of feeling in Anne's heart. 'Her eye half met Captain Wentworth's. A bow, a courtesy passed; she heard his voice; he talked to Mary, said all that was right, said something to the Miss Musgroves, enough to mark an easy footing; the room seemed full, full of persons and voices, but a few minutes ended it' (VII). The scene at the White Hart when Captain Wentworth writes his letter to Anne while she stands nearby with Captain Harville is equally dramatic, and there are many others of the same quality.

Contrast is frequently used with great effect in all the novels, and in *Persuasion* we have many excellent examples. Captain Benwick's rather sentimental sorrow for the death of his fiancée, a sorrow soon consoled by Louisa Musgrove, is contrasted with the loyal – and lasting – devotion of Captain Harville; Mary's snobbishness is contrasted with that of Elizabeth, and Sir Walter's family pride with the lack of it in Mr Elliot.

It is true to say that much of the perfection of Jane Austen's work comes from the polished style which she developed with considerable care and patience.

Humour

It has been said that the three greatest writers of comedy in English are Congreve, the seventeenth-century dramatist,

Meredith, the nineteenth-century novelist and poet, and Jane Austen. She is a great comic writer as distinct from a writer of humour. This question of the difference between humour which is comedy, and what is usually called humour, is very difficult, and perhaps the best way to distinguish them is to say that comedy comes from the intellect while humour springs from the emotions. Dickens was a great writer of humour; he makes us laugh with Mr Pickwick and a hundred others, and then because his appeal is to our emotions, he can pass immediately to pathos, so that our laughter turns to tears. Comedy is quite different, and Shakespeare, who was a master of both humour and comedy, gives an excellent example of it in the character of Malvolio in *Twelfth Night*. We laugh at Malvolio, not with him, and the joke is the incongruity between what he thinks of himself and what we see him to be. Jane Austen's humour is largely of this comic kind; she sees how absurd is the contrast between Sir Walter Elliot's vanity about his rank and his appearance and the man himself, stupid and emptyheaded, and she makes the reader laugh at him. We all know someone like Mrs Musgrove, talkative and boring, even if kind-hearted, and in real life we should not find her amusing, but Jane Austen makes us find her funny because she exaggerates her smugness and self-satisfaction.

Jane Austen often uses quiet irony to suggest much more than she actually says; for example, when Anne mentions to her father and sister that she has already seen Mr Elliot at Lyme, we are told, 'They could not listen to her description of him. They were describing him themselves; Sir Walter especially.' What a great deal of meaning is contained in those few words! Again, when the relations between Henrietta and Louisa and their cousins at Winthrop are first mentioned, she tells us that the two families were on excellent terms, with no pride or envy between them, and 'only such a consciousness of superiority in the Miss Musgroves as made them pleased to improve their cousins' (IX), a statement which implies a wealth of information about the two girls.

Most of the humour, or comedy, is that of character rather than of situation. Quite frequently she dislikes the people of whom she makes fun and disapproves of their faults, yet her satire is seldom bitter. The satirist, like the writer of comedy, sees the faults in people and has an intense desire to correct them, so he often lashes out in a way which may make the reader laugh but which, at the same time, makes those against whom the satire is directed feel very uncomfortable and angry. In *Gulliver's Travels*, for example, we laugh at the idea of politicians being chosen for office because of their skill in balancing on a tightrope, but Robert Walpole and the other politicians of Swift's day were furious when they recognized how apt was the satire. Jane Austen's satire is always quiet and subtle, however, for she never loses sympathy with her characters, stupid and boring though they may be. Her novels show the comedy of life of a small circle of English society, the upper middle class of the south of England.

Suitability for radio, stage and cinema

Persuasion has been very successfully adapted as a radio serial. Jane Austen's books lend themselves admirably to this medium since they depend so much on the interplay of character and upon atmosphere. It is possible to introduce the authoress herself as commentator or narrator, thus giving an intimate, friendly effect, and as she was so quick to judge a character and so witty in her summing up, the narration is as attractive and gives as much scope to an actress as the dialogue. The excellence of the character drawing makes the listener become interested in the people of the book and regard them as real friends, while the gentle pace of the story and the pleasant life depicted are ideal for the purposes of radio drama. The books are particularly suitable for adaptation as serials, of course, since they deal with the day to day life of the characters, and the things that happen are mostly the trivial events which occur in the lives of the average man or woman even today. Trivial as they are, however, Jane Austen contrives to make them interesting and even exciting. *Persuasion* is even better on the radio than the other books, because Anne Elliot is more sympathetically presented than any of the other heroines.

Persuasion has been less frequently adapted for the stage than the other novels of Jane Austen, probably because the characters are less exaggerated. The love story of Anne and Captain

Wentworth, which is the main theme of the book, is a quiet, personal affair, not at all spectacular, and yet it has its moments of intense emotion and it would be possible to represent on the stage the first meeting of Anne with the man she gave up seven years before, the comedy of Captain Wentworth's apparent interest in Louisa and Henrietta Musgrove, and the final understanding of the lovers. Anne would be a charming heroine and Wentworth a dashing hero. Much of the success of the play would depend on the humour, particularly of character. The parts of Mrs Musgrove, Sir Walter and Admiral Croft would give great scope to experienced players, while the sly Mrs Clay, the objectionable Mr Elliot, the faithful Captain Harville and the fickle Captain Benwick are so well contrasted that they would be a delight to watch. The constumes of the period are quaint and should offer a further attraction. Above all, the dialogue is so good that much of it could be transferred to the stage with little alteration.

The book could be more easily adapted as a film than as a play, however, since it depends so much upon atmosphere. The spacious houses of the early nineteenth century, the spreading lawns and neat ordered gardens, the elegance and beauty of the city of Bath, then at the zenith of its popularity, would provide a pleasant setting against which the story could be played. Plenty of contrast could be provided by showing the Cobb on a bright autumn day, the night of misty rain when Anne waited for Lady Russell's carriage, the warmth and brightness of the Concert Rooms and the darkness and poverty of Mrs Smith's bedroom at Bath. Many of the significant incidents, such as Anne's unintentional eavesdropping during the autumn walk and her meeting with Admiral Croft in Gay Street when he criticized the print of a ship in the window of the book-shop, could be represented in film, when they would be out of place on the stage. The plot is simple and interesting, the characters are all well defined, and there is plenty of pleasant humour, so that, all things considered, it could make a delightful film.

The novel before Jane Austen

Although the roots of the English novel go back to the sixteenth century, this form of literature did not really come to full growth until the eighteenth. In the time of Elizabeth I several writers produced pleasant stories about kings or courtiers in romantic settings such as Sir Philip Sidney's *Arcadia*, and those of Thomas Lodge and Robert Greene, from which Shakespeare took the plots of *As You Like It* and *The Winter's Tale*. At the same time Thomas Deloney was writing stories of real life, *Thomas of Reading*, *Jack of Newberry* and *The Gentle Craft*, which deal with the lives of weavers, shoe-makers and the like. But none of these can justly be termed a novel. In the seventeenth century there came other books, notably Bunyan's *Pilgrim's Progress*, which told exciting stories in realistic settings and so helped in the development of the novel form, although they, too, were not actual novels. These were followed in the early eighteenth century by the works of Daniel Defoe and Dean Swift, which also prepared the way. Finally, in 1740, *Pamela or Virtue Rewarded*, by Samuel Richardson, appeared, and the novel form was established. *Pamela* was written in the form of letters, and many of the novels which followed were also in this rather clumsy form. Richardson found his book so popular that he went on to write others, *Clarissa or the History of a Young Lady* and *Sir Charles Grandison*, both dealing with everyday people in whom one can believe. After Richardson came Henry Fielding, whose first novel, *The History of the Adventures of Joseph Andrews and his friend, Abraham Adams*, set out to make fun of Richardson's work, so it is said, but ended as a novel in its own right. He is most famous for *Tom Jones*, one of the greatest picaresque novels ever written. Soon a whole group of people was writing in English, including Tobias Smollett, from whom we have *Roderick Random*, *Peregrine Pickle* and the very amusing *Adventures of Humphrey Clinker*, and Lawrence Sterne, whose greatest novel, *The Life and Opinions of Tristram Shandy* is a masterpiece, although written in a difficult style. The form appealed especially to women, and in 1778 there appeared anonymously a book called *Evelina or the History of a Young Lady's Entry into the World*. This was the work of Fanny Burney, who afterwards wrote *Cecilia*, referred to by Jane Austen in *Persuasion*. These, like the novels of Maria Edgeworth, which came a little later, and those of Jane Austen herself, were concerned with real people in everyday circumstances. There were other novelists writing in quite a different way, with absurd plots and extraordinary, even impossible adventures. Horace Walpole's *Castle of Otranto*, published in 1764, began the vogue, but the most successful writer of this type of book was Mrs Ann Radcliffe, whose five novels were greatly admired, and whose *Mysteries of Udolpho*, with its Gothic castle, its gloomy and morose villain, its frightened heroine, influenced prose-writers and poets alike. Jane Austen and her sister read many of these earlier novels, and *Northanger Abbey*, probably Jane's earliest novel, makes fun of these tales of terror. This was the background against which Jane Austen wrote and one reason she came so near to perfection was that she read the work of her predecessors so intelligently and was able to learn so much from them.

Notes

Chapter I

Sir Walter Elliot of Kellynch Hall in Somerset has three daughters; Elizabeth, who, like her father, is handsome and vain and is spoiled by him, Anne, of whom her father has no great opinion, and Mary, who is married to Charles Musgrove. When the story opens, in 1814, their mother has been dead for thirteen years, and during this time her friend, Lady Russell, has tried to advise them. Elizabeth once wished to marry William Walter Elliot, a cousin, who will succeed to the family title and estates on her father's death, but he had married someone else. Sir Walter is now deeply in debt.

patents written documents under the king's seal conveying the title of baronet; short for Letters Patent.

endless creations of the last century Many men were given the title of baronet in the eighteenth century during political intrigues.

Dugdale Sir William Dugdale compiled *The Baronage of England* in 1675–6.

Baronet Title invented by James I in 1611 and sold for £1,050. Next in rank below a baron. The title is hereditary.

quarto next in size to folio page, i.e. a sheet of paper folded twice.

heir presumptive He was Sir Walter's nearest male relative and so it was presumed he would succeed. If Sir Walter married again, however, and had a son, the child would have a better claim and would be the heir apparent.

awful legacy Note the correct use of the word 'awful'. The care of three daughters might well cause a father to be 'full of awe'.

worsting growing worse. An old form.

crow's foot wrinkle.

solicited asked in marriage, proposed to.

book of books *The Baronetage*, giving details of all the baronets in England and their families.

Tattersall's Club for racing men and place where racehorses were sold by auction. The place was established near Hyde Park Corner in London by Richard Tattersall in 1766.

black ribbons These showed that she was in mourning.

taking no present to Anne Note Elizabeth's character.
alienable saleable. Most of his estate belonged to him only for life; he could not dispose of it as he wished.
to mortgage to allow a creditor to have possession of property as security for money lent.

Chapter II

Mr Shepherd, Sir Walter's agent, and Lady Russell are consulted about ways of saving money. Eventually Sir Walter agrees to live in Bath and Mr Shepherd is told that if he is asked by a suitable person for permission to rent Kellynch, he may let the house. Lady Russell disapproves of Elizabeth's friendship with Mr Shepherd's daughter, Mrs Clay.

knight next in rank below a baronet. A knight cannot pass on his title to his heir.
She consulted Anne Note Anne's character.
whose interest was involved in the reality Mr Shepherd's own fees could not be paid unless Sir Walter really began to retrench.

Chapter III

Mr Shepherd suggests that since many naval officers are leaving the Service with large fortunes, obtained from the capture of enemy ships, one of them might be a suitable tenant for Kellynch. Sir Walter objects, but later on, when Admiral Croft enquires about renting the house, he is persuaded to accept him as a tenant. Anne is agitated when she hears that Mrs Croft is a relative of Mr Wentworth, who was once curate at Monkford.

peace Peace of Paris, 1814, ending the Napoleonic Wars.
rich naval officers Many sailors made fortunes from prize money, the value of the merchant ships and men-of-war which they captured.
neat and careful Sailors must be this because of their cramped quarters.
dab of powder To cover and hide his baldness.
chusing An old form of the word.
personableness attractiveness.
quarter sessions Local courts to try civil and criminal cases, held quarterly by the Justices of the Peace in a county and by the Recorder in some boroughs.

rear-admiral of the white There are four ranks of admiral in the British Navy: Admiral of the Fleet, Admiral, Vice-Admiral and Rear-Admiral, which is the lowest. Until 1865 these ranks were sub-divided into those of the red, white and blue squadrons. Note Jane Austen's accuracy; she had two brothers who became admirals.

You misled me by the term 'gentleman' The lower orders of clergy were treated as superior servants in the eighteenth century, when each great house had its own chaplain.

Chapter IV

This chapter explains that seven years previously Anne was engaged to Captain Frederick Wentworth, brother of the curate. Her father and Lady Russell did not approve because he had no fortune, and Anne was persuaded to break the engagement.

action off St. Domingo Fought during Nelson's pursuit of the French fleet to the West Indies in 1805, just before Trafalgar.

have a ship to be given command of a ship.

station port to which a warship is posted.

Navy lists Giving the names of the ships and officers of the Navy for each year.

Chapter V

Admiral and Mrs Croft agree to take Kellynch. Sir Walter and his daughters are to live in Bath, where Elizabeth wishes Mrs Clay to accompany them. Anne, who is afraid that her father may marry this woman, protests against the arrangement, but to no purpose. Anne stays for a time with Lady Russell, and later goes to her sister, Mary Musgrove, at Uppercross. Mary's whims and the good-humour of her sisters-in-law, the Misses Henrietta and Louisa Musgrove, are described.

This indenture sheweth The first words on the legal agreement between Sir Walter and his tenant. Originally such an agreement was written in duplicate on the same piece of paper or parchment which was then torn in halves; the indentations of the torn paper would fit exactly, hence the word 'indenture'.

afflicted tenantry They were going to lose Sir Walter and were supposed to be sad in consequence.

Revision questions on chapters I-V

1 What was Sir Walter Elliot's favourite occupation and what light does it throw upon his character?

2 Give a brief description of Elizabeth and Anne Elliot and of Mary Musgrove.

3 How are the different characters of the three sisters suggested in these early chapters?

4 What was Sir Walter's opinion of naval officers, and how was he at last persuaded to let Kellynch to Admiral Croft?

5 What suggestions are made about the character of Mrs Clay? Do you think Anne was justified in her suspicions of this woman?

6 Describe the village of Uppercross.

7 What do you learn from these chapters about Lady Russell?

Chapter VI

Anne spends a tolerably pleasant time at Uppercross, visiting Mary's relatives by marriage at the Great House and listening to confidences from everyone. While she is there, Admiral and Mrs Croft pay their first neighbourly call. Anne learns that Captain Wentworth is in England and about to visit his sister, Mrs Croft. Mrs Musgrove, Mary's mother-in-law, discovers that Captain Wentworth was in command of the ship in which her ne'er-do-well son, now dead, once served.

the precedence that was her due As the daughter of a baronet Mary was entitled to leave the dining-room before the ladies who were of lower rank. Note the insistence upon rank in the novel.

Chapter VII

Anne dreads meeting Captain Wentworth and at first she is able to avoid him. Mary's little boy has a bad fall, which causes his parents and Anne some anxiety, so that she has an excuse for not dining at the Great House when the captain is expected. At last, however, he comes to the Cottage and for a brief moment she sees him again. Charles Musgrove's young sisters are delighted with him. Mary tells Anne that he has said she 'is so altered that he would not have known her'. Anne feels that this is a reference to the loss of her youthful beauty and is deeply hurt.

apothecary The equivalent of the modern pharmacist, but he also acted as surgeon.

Chapter VIII

Anne and Captain Wentworth meet frequently. A typical evening at the Great House is described with Mrs Musgrove questioning Captain Wentworth about her son and Anne playing for the dancing.

pelisse a long cloak, with or without sleeves.
Sound Plymouth Sound.
Great Nation the French; this was their name for themselves.
I have lived . . . war It was the custom of the wives and families of naval officers to travel from port to port on the ship. Some women lived on board for considerable periods.

Chapter IX

Charles Hayter, a curate and Mrs Musgrove's sister's son, returns after a short absence. He is in love with Henrietta who, he believed, returned his affection. He now finds that she is very interested in Captain Wentworth. Both he and Wentworth chance to visit Mary's cottage at the same time. Walter, the eldest child, climbs on Anne's back as she kneels beside the invalid. Charles Hayter orders him to get down, but Captain Wentworth removes him.

Chapter X

Anne cannot decide whether Frederick Wentworth favours Henrietta or Louisa. One morning in November the whole party, Captain Wentworth, Mary, Charles, Anne, Louisa and Henrietta go for a long walk, during which Mary behaves badly, complaining of everything. They arrive, by Henrietta's and Louisa's planning, near Winthrop, the home of the Hayters. Henrietta and her brother go down to the house while the others remain at the top of the hill. Anne overhears Louisa telling Captain Wentworth that Charles Musgrove proposed to her, Anne, before he married Mary and that she refused him. When

Henrietta returns, she brings Charles Hayter with her and they seem to have made up their quarrel. The party meets Admiral and Mrs Croft, and Wentworth shows great thoughtfulness in seeing that Anne is given the vacant seat in their gig.

lieve lief, rather; the old form.

Revision questions on chapters VI-X

1 What is Mary Musgrove's opinion of her mother-in-law, and Mrs Musgrove's opinion of Mary, as expressed to Anne?

2 Describe life at Uppercross.

3 Why did Anne fear meeting Captain Wentworth? How did she avoid the meeting at first and how did it eventually take place?

4 Give a description of Admiral and Mrs Croft.

5 Why was Mrs Musgrove particularly interested in Captain Wentworth? Describe the conversation between them.

6 Give an account of the November walk. What was its importance?

7 Who were the Hayters? Give some account of them.

Chapter XI

Anne prepares to return to Lady Russell. Captain Wentworth absents himself from Uppercross for a while and, when he comes back, explains that he has been to see his friend, Captain Harville, at Lyme. The Musgrove girls wish to visit the place so Charles, Mary, Anne and Captain Wentworth set out with them. They are charmed with Lyme, where they are to spend the night. They meet Captain Benwick, who is, apparently, heartbroken because Captain's Harville's sister, to whom he was engaged, has recently died. Anne tries to help him to overcome his grief.

Lyme Lyme Regis, a watering place in Dorset on the shores of the English Channel. Monmouth landed here in 1685.
curricle two-wheeled chaise drawn by two horses abreast.
rooms Assembly Rooms, where dances and concerts were held.

Cobb Very old, curved stone pier at Lyme Regis.
falling of the cliff Landslides are frequent along this coast.
Marmion* or *The Lady of the Lake Long narrative poems by Sir Walter Scott. He won his reputation by his poetry, but when the poems of Lord Byron first appeared and he recognized that they were superior to his own, he turned to writing novels (see p.iv).
The Giaour* and *The Bride of Abydos Poems by Lord Byron.

Chapter XII

Next morning, while the party is walking through Lyme, they meet a gentleman who glances with admiration at Anne. Enquiry at the inn shows that he is Mr Elliot, heir to Sir Walter's title and estates. When they enquire, he has just left for Bath and London. Louisa meets with an accident on the Cobb and injures her head. Charles suggests that Anne should stay with her while the others return to Uppercross to break the news to Mr and Mrs Musgrove.

procuring a dispensation obtaining the bishop's permission to live out of his parish.
Cape Cape of Good Hope.
run up to the yard arm put to death by being hanged from the cross spar, as mutineers and other offenders were.
Byron's 'dark blue seas' Misquotation from Byron's *Childe Harold.*
an Emma towards her Henry Allusion to the ballad, *Henry and Emma*, by the eighteenth-century poet, Matthew Prior; it was an adaptation of the old medieval ballad, *The Nut-Brown Maid.*
baited refreshed, rested.

Chapter XIII

After spending two days with Louisa's parents at Uppercross, and learning from Charles, Mary's husband, and Charles Hayter, that Louisa is no worse, although still very ill, Anne persuades the whole Musgrove family to go to Lyme, where Captain Wentworth is already established. She, herself, then travels to Lady Russell's house. She is amazed to find that her interest in her father and sister has become secondary to her interest in the Musgroves. With Lady Russell she visits Kellynch, where she learns that the Crofts are going away to visit relatives in the north.

Chapter XIV

Charles and Mary bring news from Lyme to Anne and Lady Russell. Louisa is recovering, although she must still remain at Lyme for some time. Mary has found much to displease her, including Captain Benwick's obvious admiration for Anne. Mr and Mrs Musgrove return home to welcome the younger members of their family for Christmas. Lady Russell dislikes the noise of the children at Uppercross, but finds the noises of Bath agreeable when she and Anne arrive there. Anne learns that Mr Elliot has called upon her father.

given Mrs Musgrove precedence Note Mary's insistence on rank.

pattens wooden soles on an iron ring, used to keep the boot or shoe from the ground in wet or muddy weather.

Chapter XV

Anne arrives at her father's house in Camden Place and is given news of his social activities and those of her sister. She hears much of Mr Elliot, who has made a great impression on Sir Walter. Anne thinks that he may wish to marry Elizabeth. Later she meets him and he is obviously glad to see her again. Mrs Clay is still with Elizabeth.

having cards left Strict etiquette was observed in Jane Austen's time. When newcomers came to a district, the neighbours called and left visiting cards.

under-hung with a projecting lower jaw.

watchman Men were employed to patrol the streets of the towns at night to proclaim the hours and the state of the weather, and to keep order.

Revision questions on chapters XI-XV

1 Explain why Captain Benwick is staying with the Harvilles. What is your first impression of him?

2 What is the Cobb? What picture of Lyme do you get from Jane Austen's description of it?

3 Describe Anne's first conversation with Captain Benwick.

4 What were the immediate results of Louisa's accident?

5 When did Anne first notice Mr Elliot? Describe the incident.

6 Give an account of the visit of Anne and Lady Russell to Uppercross at Christmas time.

7 Describe Anne's first evening with her father and sister in Bath.

8 What impression have you formed of the character of Lady Russell?

Chapter XVI

At first Anne worries about the possibility of a marriage between her father and Mrs Clay, but as time goes on, she becomes so pleased with the friendship of Mr Elliot, who, she imagines, is desirous of marrying Elizabeth, that she refuses to be distressed by the idea. She is disgusted by the obsequious attitude of her father when their distant relatives, the Dowager-Viscountess Dalrymple and her daughter, arrive in Bath and take a house in Laura Place.

Gowland English form of the name Goulard. Thomas Goulard was a famous French surgeon of Charles II's time who made a lotion for the complexion which was much used by the ladies of the eighteenth century. It contained bitter almonds and bichloride of mercury.
a little learning is by no means a dangerous thing Misquotation from Pope's *Essay on Criticism.*

Chapter XVII

Anne learns from a former governess that an old schoolfellow, now Mrs Smith, who had befriended her in childhood, is staying in Bath in difficult circumstances. She is a widow, poor and crippled by rheumatic fever. Anne goes to visit her and is impressed by her courage and cheerfulness. One day Anne forgoes a visit to Laura Place because she has promised to go to her friend, and is rebuked by her father in consequence. Lady Russell is convinced that as soon as Mr Elliot's period of mourning for his wife is over, he will propose to Anne, but Anne is beginning to judge his character and is not very satisfied with what she observes.

au fait up-to-date, in the swim.

Chapter XVIII

Anne receives a letter from Mary, which has been brought to Bath by Admiral and Mrs Croft, who are visiting the city because the admiral has gout. Mary tells of Louisa Musgrove's recovery and of her return to Uppercross. During her convalescence at Lyme she has fallen in love with Captain Benwick, and they are engaged. Anne meets Admiral Croft, who tells her that Frederick Wentworth does not seem upset by this engagement, and say he must persuade the captain to visit Bath.

I do not think they improve as neighbours . . . a pleasant family Note Mary's fickle nature.

peace See note p.40.

younker young fellow.

piano mild, soft.

Chapter XIX

Captain Wentworth comes to Bath, and Anne meets him by chance when she and her party are caught in the rain. Elizabeth ignores him. He is obviously embarrassed at seeing Anne. She has a conversation with him which lasts until Mr Elliot comes to escort her home. After this meeting she is constantly watching for him and her manner is sometimes so confused that her friend, Mrs Smith, suspects her of being in love.

barouche roomy four-wheeled carriage with a folding top.

chair sedan chair. A special small type was used in Bath.

Chapter XX

The Elliots attend a concert which is patronized by Lady Dalrymple. While they are waiting for her to arrive, Anne sees Captain Wentworth and speaks to him. From the conversation she gathers that he may still be in love with her. During the concert Mr Elliot makes it clear that he wishes to marry her, and this distresses her. When she succeeds in talking with Captain Wentworth again, Mr Elliot interrupts, whereupon the captain wishes her 'goodnight', and she realizes with consternation that he is jealous.

concert bill programme. This would be a very large piece of paper, closely printed in bad ink.

gapes yawns.
Miss Larolles Character in the eighteenth-century novel *Cecilia*, by Fanny Burney.

Revision questions on chapters XVI-XX

1 What does the arrival of the Dowager-Viscountess Dalrymple reveal about the characters of the various members of the Elliot family?

2 Tell Mrs Smith's story and describe Anne's first visit to her.

3 Who was Nurse Rooke and what do you know of her?

4 What does Mary's letter to Anne tell you about Mary's character?

5 Write a detailed account of Anne's meeting with Admiral Croft in Milsom Street.

6 Describe fully the concert which was patronized by Lady Dalrymple.

7 Write a short account of the city of Bath as described by Jane Austen.

Chapter XXI

On the morning after the concert Anne visits Mrs Smith, who makes it quite clear that she thinks Anne will eventually marry Mr Elliot. When Anne denies this possibility, Mrs Smith reveals that she has known Mr Elliot for many years, as he was a friend of her late husband. She tells Anne how despicable he is, for he married his first wife for her money and is now friendly with Sir Walter only because he wishes to prevent him from marrying Mrs Clay, since, if Sir Walter should marry again and a son should be born, Mr Elliot would lose the title. Anne is indignant about all this, especially when she learns that Mr Elliot has also refused to help Mrs Smith to obtain her husband's estates in the West Indies, which would bring her a much larger income.

sequestration seizing of property by the State in compensation for taxes due.

Chapter XXII

Anne is very worried about what she has learned of Mr Elliot and determines to consult Lady Russell. On arrival home she discovers that she has missed Mr Elliot's call, as she hoped, but that he is calling again in the evening, since he is to visit friends at Thornberry Park the next day. Anne treats him very coolly when he comes. Next morning, as she is about to set out for Lady Russell's house, Mary and her husband arrive unexpectedly. They have come to Bath with Mrs Musgrove, Henrietta and Captain Harville. Henrietta is to buy clothes since she is soon to marry Charles Hayter, who has been given a temporary living not far from Uppercross. Anne goes to visit Mrs Musgrove and meets Frederick Wentworth again. Mary sees Mr Elliot, who is supposed to be at Thornberry, talking with Mrs Clay in the street. Charles books a box at the theatre for the next evening, but is obliged to cancel it since Sir Walter and Elizabeth invite them all to an evening party at Camden Place. Anne hopes that Frederick Wentworth will realize that she is not in love with Mr Elliot. When she returns home, she tells Mrs Clay that she has been talking to Mr Elliot, whereupon the lady makes excuses.

spell angle, fish for.

hold a living for a youth Most great families had a living in the Church which the head of the family could bestow on whom he pleased. In this case he intended it for a boy who would not be old enough to carry out the duties for some years, and Charles was asked to do the work temporarily.

Pump Room Place where the medicinal waters are served.

Chapter XXIII

Next day Anne visits the Musgroves again and finds several people, including Frederick Wentworth, already there. While Mrs Musgrove is giving Mrs Croft an account of her various emotions concerning Henrietta and Charles Hayter, Captain Harville talks to Anne and tells her that he has been commissioned by Captain Benwick to have a miniature of himself set so that it could be worn. This painting had been intended originally for Captain Harville's sister, but is now to be given to Louisa. Captain Harville is rather upset by Benwick's engagement and talks for some time about it to Anne, who declares that women are more faithful than men to those whom they can never hope to marry. Captain Wentworth has undertaken to deal with the miniature for Harville and he is, apparently, writing a letter about it. Later, however, he gives Anne a second letter in which he declares his continuing love for her and asks for some kind of sign to show her feelings. She tries to find some way of seeing him to give the sign, but finds many difficulties. At last she sets out for Camden Place escorted by Charles, who, when they meet Wentworth, asks him to escort her, as he, Charles, wishes to visit the gunsmith. At last the lovers come to an understanding and are happy.

Sultaness Scheherazade She tells the tales in *The Arabian Nights.*
analogy comparison, likeness, resemblance.
good anchorage Note the nautical metaphor.
an alloy in Her happiness was strengthened by a few momentary worries just as precious metal is strengthened by the baser metal mixed with it.

Chapter XXIV

This chapter relates in brief all that happened later. Captain Wentworth and Anne were married, with Sir Walter's blessing. Lady Russell was at last won over to approve of Anne's husband. Mary was very pleased although she did not like Anne's right to take precedence of her. Elizabeth was disappointed in her hopes of a marriage with Mr Elliot, for he soon went away, followed a little later by Mrs Clay.

volume of honour *The Baronetage.*

Revision questions on chapters XXI-XXIV

1 What was Mrs Smith's estimate of Mr Elliot's character?

2 Describe the unexpected arrival of Mrs Musgrove and her friends in Bath.

3 Give an account of Anne's difficulties after she has read Captain Wentworth's letter.

4 Give an account in your own words of the conversation of (a) Mrs Musgrove and Mrs Croft, and (b) Anne and Captain Harville, when Anne visited Mrs Musgrove at her hotel.

5 What does Jane Austen tell us about the later lives of her characters?

6 Why did Elizabeth change her opinion of Captain Wentworth and what effect did this have?

7 Describe the card party given by Sir Walter and Elizabeth on the night after the arrival of the Musgroves in Bath.

General questions

1 What are the chief points which you would consider in criticizing a novel? Illustrate by references to *Persuasion*.

2 Do you think, after reading this novel, that Jane Austen was a snob?

3 What have you learned from this book about the life of women in the early nineteenth century?

4 It has been said that one could never imagine the naval officers who are introduced into *Persuasion* to have come from fighting Napoleon's navy. Do you agree with this criticism?

5 What have you learned from this book about the Navy of the early nineteenth century?

6 Would you like to have lived in Jane Austen's world or not? Give reasons for your answer.

7 'Bath is a city of contrasts. Opulence and poverty are to be found side by side.' Show how Jane Austen confirms this statement.

8 What are your impressions of Lyme Regis as gathered from this book?

9 'Most of the characters in this novel are obsessed with the idea of rank.' Do you consider this statement to be true? Discuss it.

10 Why did Mr Elliot go to Bath? What effect did his arrival there have (a) upon Elizabeth, and (b) upon Mrs Clay?

11 'The events which take place at Lyme are the most important in the story.' Do you agree? What effect have these events upon the life of Anne Elliot?

12 What is the importance in the novel of (a) Captain Benwick's miniature, and (b) Mr Elliot's curricle?

13 Show, from incidents in the story, (a) what Lady Russell finds to praise in Mr Elliot, and (b) what Mrs Smith finds to censure in him.

14 Describe in detail three incidents (from different parts of the story) in which Anne is distressed.

15 Who was 'poor Dick'? How does he figure in the story?

16 Jane Austen has been accused of being cruel to some of her characters. Do you think this applies to any of those in *Persuasion*?

17 What do the three letters in this novel tell you about the people who wrote them?

18 What characteristics have the sailors in *Persuasion* in common? How do they differ from each other?

19 What is your opinion of Mrs Smith? Do you think her character is well drawn?

20 Discuss Jane Austen's knowledge of human nature with especial reference to Elizabeth and Mary.

21 Have you any sympathy for Mrs Clay? Describe her part in the story.

22 Jane Austen had many nieces and nephews. From your reading of *Persuasion* do you think she understood children?

23 Which of the characters in the novel would you most like to meet and why?

24 Do you consider that Charles Musgrove was unfortunate in his choice of a wife?

25 Contrast Anne's emotions (a) as she leaves Kellynch, and (b) as she enters Bath.

26 Why does Captain Wentworth refer to his friend as 'poor Harville'? Do you consider that this is an apt description of him? Give reasons for your answer.

27 'Sir Walter Elliot is one of the amusing characters of English Literature.' Discuss this statement.

28 Lady Russell and Mrs Croft are both sensible women. Do you consider that they are made attractive to the reader? Which of them do you prefer?

29 Jane Austen shows great skill in dialogue. Illustrate this by an account of two conversations in the book.

30 What are the chief points about the style of the novel which impress you?

31 'Jane Austen could describe places as well as she could judge people.' Mention some of the descriptions in *Persuasion* which you think to be especially good, and say briefly why you think them so.

32 Illustrate from this story Jane Austen's humour in describing a character.

33 Do you think *Persuasion* could be made into a play? Which incidents would you use if you dramatized it?

34 If you tried to adapt *Persuasion* as a film, do you think your work would be difficult?

35 What is there about *Persuasion* which makes it suitable for adaptation as a radio play or serial? How would you suggest doing this?

36 Write notes on the following: Tattersall's, the Cobb, curricle, watchman, 'an Emma towards her Henry,' Miss Larolles, sequestration, Sultaness Scheherazade, *The Giaour*. How are they mentioned in the book?

Context questions

Answer briefly the questions below each of the following passages:

1 I mean to go with you, – for I am of no more use at home than you are. If I were to shut myself up for ever with the child, I should not be able to persuade him to do anything he did not like.

a) On what occasion were these words spoken and by whom?
b) Fill in the blank with the name of the person spoken to.
c) What does the passage show about the speaker's character?
d) How was the difficulty solved?

2 Upon all points of blood and connexion he is a completely altered man. Having long had as much money as he could spend, nothing to wish for on the side of avarice and indulgence, he has been gradually learning to pin his happiness upon the consequence he is heir to.

a) Who is the speaker and to whom is he or she speaking?
b) Who is the person referred to?
c) Explain why this person had changed his attitude.
d) Express the meaning of the second sentence of the passage in your own words.

3 The breakfast-room chimney smokes a little, I grant you, but it is only when the wind is due north and blows hard, which may not happen three times a winter.

a) Who is the speaker and whom is he addressing?
b) Why might the occasion on which these words were spoken be a painful one for the person addressed?
c) What changes has the speaker made in the house he is talking about?

4 How many days was it, my dear, between the first time of my seeing you and our sitting down together in our lodgings at North Yarmouth?

a) Who is asking this question and of whom?
b) Describe the occasion.
c) Why does the speaker remember his or her past at this time?

5 And she declined on her own account with great alacrity – 'She was engaged to spend the evening with an old schoolfellow.'

a) What was the invitation which was declined and who declined it?
b) Who was the old schoolfellow?
c) Briefly tell her story.
d) Why did the person spoken of decline 'with great alacrity'?

6 He did justice to his very gentleman-like appearance, his air of elegance and fashion, his good-shaped face, his sensible eye; but at the same time 'must lament his being much under-hung, a defect which time seemed to have increased; nor could he pretend to say that ten years had not altered almost every feature for the worse.'

a) Of whom is this a description and who gave it?
b) Why had the two people not met for ten years?
c) What does this passage tell you about the person who gives the description?
d) Explain 'under-hung'.

7 I knew pretty well what she was before that day . . . I had no more discoveries to make than you would have as to the fashion and strength of any old pelisse, which you had seen lent about among half your acquaintance ever since you could remember, and which at last, on some very wet day, is lent to yourself. Ah! she was a dear old Asp to me.

a) Who is the speaker and to whom is he speaking?
b) Describe the occasion.
c) What was the 'Asp'?
d) Explain 'pelisse'.

8 I have done something for you that you will like. I have been to the theatre and secured a box for to-morrow night. Ain't I a good boy? I know you love a play and there is room for us all.

a) Who is the 'good boy'?
b) Who is he addressing and on what occasion?
c) Who are the people he proposes to take to the theatre?
d) Who objects to his plan and why?

9 And having talked of poetry, the richness of the present age, and gone through a brief comparison of opinion as to the first-rate poets, trying to ascertain whether *Marmion* or *The Lady of the Lake* were to be preferred, and how ranked *The Giaour* and *The Bride of Abydos* . . . he showed himself so intimately acquainted with all the tenderest songs of one poet, and all the impassioned descriptions of hopeless agony of the other . . . that she ventured to hope he did not always read only poetry.

a) Describe the circumstances in which this conversation about poetry took place.
b) Why was one of the people concerned especially interested in poetry?
c) In the light of events which followed, what is your opinion of this person's interest in poetry?
d) Name the authors of the poems mentioned.

10 Oh ay! Mr. —, the curate of Monkford. You misled me by the term 'gentleman'. I thought you were speaking of some man of property: Mr. — was nobody, I remember; quite unconnected; nothing to do with the Stafford family.

a) Who is speaking and on what occasion?
b) Fill in the name of the person under discussion.
c) What does this passage indicate about the character of the speaker?
d) Explain 'quite unconnected'.

The following plain context questions will be found useful for revision. Connect the passages with their contexts, identify the speakers and add comments on any points of interest.

11 To look forward and see you occupying your dear mother's place, succeeding to all her rights . . . would be the highest possible gratification to me.

12 I have known a great deal of the profession; and besides their liberality, they are so neat and careful in all their ways.

13 Will it not be wiser to accept the society of these good ladies in Laura Place, and enjoy all the advantage of the connexion as far as possible?

14 No, no, it is not man's nature. I will not allow it to be more man's nature than woman's to be inconstant and forget those they do love, or have loved.

15 I hate to hear of women on board, or to see them on board.

16 For heaven's sake go to him. I can support her myself. Leave me and go to him.

17 That tooth of hers and those freckles! Freckles do not disgust me so much as they do him.

18 She had gone to her letters, and found it all as she supposed; and the re-perusal of these letters, after so long an interval . . . had affected her spirits exceedingly.

19 If I thought it would not tempt her to go out in sharp winds and grow coarse, I would send her a new hat and pelisse.

20 He begged her pardon, but she must be applied to, to explain Italian again.

Key to context questions

1 VII; **2** XXI; **3** XIII; **4** X; **5** XVII; **6** XV; **7** VIII; **8** XXII; **9** XI; **10** III; **11** XVII; **12** III; **13** XVI; **14** XXIII; **15** VIII; **16** XII; **17** V; **18** VI; **19** XV; **20** XX.